Claire Thacker and Cheryl Pelteret

with Herbert Puchta and Jeff Stranks

English in Mind

* Teacher's Book Starter

CAMBRIDGE
UNIVERSITY PRESS

CAMBRIDGE UNIVERSITY PRESS
Cambridge, New York, Melbourne, Madrid, Cape Town, Singapore, São Paulo

Cambridge University Press
The Edinburgh Building, Cambridge CB2 8RU, UK

www.cambridge.org
Information on this title: www.cambridge.org/9780521750424

First published 2004
5th printing 2007

Printed in the United Kingdom at the University Press, Cambridge

A catalogue record for this publication is available from the British Library

ISBN 978-0-521-75042-4 Teacher's Book
ISBN 978-0-521-75038-7 Student's Book
ISBN 978-0-521-75041-7 Workbook with Audio CD / CD-ROM
ISBN 978-0-521-75043-1 Teacher's Resource Pack
ISBN 978-0-521-75044-8 Class Cassettes
ISBN 978-0-521-54503-7 Class Audio CDs

Contents

Speaking & functions	Listening	Reading	Writing
Spelling words. Exchanging phone numbers. Using classroom language.	International words. Classroom objects. The alphabet. Phone numbers.	Story: No problem.	Phone message.
Talking about nationalities & countries. Asking questions. Correcting information.	A game show.	Dialogue in a game show. Culture: Heroes and heroines.	Information about yourself.
Expressing likes & dislikes. Describing nouns.	People talking about things they like & don't like.	Interview with a singer. Story: They all want to go …	Email about your favourite band.
Talking about your family. Asking questions about habits.	Dialogue about a family.	A famous writer. Culture: British families.	Paragraph about your family.
Asking for & giving directions. Saying where things are.	People giving directions.	A great trip to London! Story: I have no idea!	Short text about your town or city.
Talking about things you've got. Describing people. Giving personal information.	Descriptions of people.	Sally or Paula? Culture: Pets in the UK.	Descriptions of friends or family members.
Ordering food in a restaurant. Talking about food.	Dialogues in a shop and a restaurant.	Would you like our special? Story: I'm really hungry!	Letter to a host family.
Talking about regular activities & daily routine. Interviewing people about TV.	Times. Interviews about TV & TV programmes.	Different lives. Culture: What British teenagers watch.	Paragraph about TV.
Describing feelings. Giving orders.	A story. A song.	Letter to a boyfriend. Story: I miss San Francisco.	Email about your friends & school.
Talking about ability.	Information about abilities of people & animals. Dialogue about sports.	We never win but we always win. Culture: Sport in British schools.	Email about sports you do.
Talking about present activities. Describing a house.	Listen to sounds & describe activities.	Dialogue about present activities. Story: I'm on my way!	Postcard to a friend.
Talking about dates & seasons. Describing people's clothes. Discussing clothes & shopping. Asking for permission.	Descriptions of what people are wearing. Shopping dialogues.	Americans love to party! Dialogues in a clothes shop. Culture: London's carnival.	Email about a festival.
Talking about past situations. Talking about dates.	Dialogue about the Beatles. Dates.	There was a man at the door. Story: Rob's wallet.	Email about a holiday.
Questionnaire about past activities.	Radio quiz about past events.	The lady with the lamp. Culture: Steve Biko – a South African hero.	Paragraph for school magazine about a famous person.
Re-telling a story. Making guesses about past or present situations.	Radio interview about Lord Lucan.	The mystery of Lord Lucan. A mystery at sea. Story: Who's Caroline?	Story about a strange place.
Describing things. Comparing people, places & objects.	Dialogue comparing life now & in the past.	Island chef cooks in L.A. Culture: UK holiday camps – then and now.	Competition entry.

Introduction

'If you can teach teenagers, you can teach anyone.' Michael Grinder

Teaching teenagers is an interesting and challenging task. A group of adolescents can be highly motivated, cooperative and fun to teach on one day, and the next day the whole group or individual students might turn out to be truly 'difficult' – the teacher might, for example, be faced with discipline problems, disruptive or provocative behaviour, a lack of motivation, or unwillingness on the students' part to do homework assigned to them.

The roots of these problems frequently lie in the fact that adolescents are going through a period of significant changes in their lives. The key challenge in the transition period between being a child and becoming an adult is the adolescent's struggle for identity – a process that requires the development of a distinct sense of who they are. A consequence of this process is that adolescents can feel threatened, and at the same time experience overwhelming emotions. They frequently try to compensate for the perceived threats with extremely rude behaviour, and try to 'hide' their emotions behind a wall of extreme outward conformity. The more individual students manage to look, talk, act and behave like the other members of their peer group, the less threatened and insecure they feel.

Insights into the causes underlying the problems might help us to understand better the complex situation our students are in. However, such insights do not automatically lead to more success in teaching. We need to react to the challenges in a professional way.[1] This includes the need to:

- select content and organise the students' learning according to their psychological needs;
- create a positive learning atmosphere;
- cater for differences in students' learning styles and intelligence(s), and facilitate the development of our students' study skills.

English in Mind has been written taking all these points into account. They have significantly influenced the choice of texts, artwork and design, the structure of the units, the typology of exercises, and the means by which students' study skills are facilitated and extended.

The importance of the content for success

There are a number of reasons why the choice of the right content has a crucial influence over success or failure in the teaching of adolescents. Teachers frequently observe that teenagers are reluctant to 'talk about themselves'. This has to do with the adolescent's need for psychological security. Consequently, the 'further away' from their own world the content of the teaching is, the more motivating and stimulating it will be for the students. The preference for psychologically remote content goes hand in hand with a fascination with extremes and realistic details. Furthermore, students love identifying with heroes and heroines, because these idols are perceived to embody the qualities needed in order to survive in a threatening world: qualities such as courage, genius, creativity and love. In the foreign language class, students can become fascinated with stories about heroes and heroines to which they can ascribe such qualities. *English in Mind* treats students as young adults, offering them a range of interesting topics and a balance between educational value and teenage interest and fun.

As Kieran Egan[1] stresses, learning in the adolescent classroom can be successfully organised by starting with something far from the students' experience, but also connected to it by some quality with which they can associate. This process of starting far from the students makes it easier for the students to become interested in the topic, and also enables the teacher finally to relate the content to the students' own world.

A positive learning atmosphere

The creation of a positive learning atmosphere largely depends on the rapport between teacher and students, and the one which students have among themselves. It requires the teacher to be a genuine, empathetic listener, and to have a number of other psychological skills. *English in Mind* supports the teacher's task of creating positive learning experiences through: clear tasks; a large number of carefully designed exercises; regular opportunities for the students to check their own work; and a learning process designed to guarantee that the students will learn to express themselves both in speaking and in writing.

Learning styles and multiple intelligences

There is significant evidence that students will be better motivated, and learn more successfully, if differences in learning styles and intelligences are taken into account in the teaching-learning process.[2] The development of a number of activities in *English in Mind* have been

---

[1] An excellent analysis of teenage development and consequences for our teaching in general can be found in Kieran Egan: *Romantic Understanding*, Routledge and Kegan Paul, New York and London, 1990. This book has had a significant influence on the thinking behind *English in Mind*, and the development of the concept of the course.

[2] See for example Eric Jensen: *Brain-Based Learning and Teaching*, Turning Point Publishing, Del Mar, CA, USA, 1995, on learning styles. An overview of the theory of multiple intelligences can be found in Howard Gardner: *Multiple Intelligences: The Theory in Practice*, Basic Books, New York 1993.

influenced by such insights, and students find frequent study tips that show them how they can better utilise their own resources.[3]

The methodology used in *English in Mind*

Skills: *English in Mind* uses a communicative, multi-skills approach to develop the students' foreign language abilities in an interesting and motivational way. A wide range of interesting text types is used to present authentic use of language, including magazine and newspaper clippings, interviews, narratives, songs and engaging photo stories.

Grammar: *English in Mind* is based on a strong grammatical syllabus and takes into account students' mixed abilities by dealing with grammar in a carefully graded way, and offering additional teaching support (see below).

Vocabulary: *English in Mind* offers a systematic vocabulary syllabus, including important lexical chunks for conversation.

Culture: *English in Mind* gives students insights into a number of important cross-cultural and intercultural themes. Significant cultural features of English-speaking countries are presented, and students are involved in actively reflecting on the similarities and differences between other cultures and their own.

Consolidation: Four Check your progress revision units per level will give teachers a clear picture of their students' progress and make students aware of what they have learned. Each revision unit is also accompanied by a project which gives students the opportunity to use new language in a less controlled context and allows for learner independence.

Teacher support: *English in Mind* is clearly structured and easy to teach. The Teacher's Book offers step-by-step lesson notes, background information on content, culture and language, additional teaching ideas and the tapescripts. The accompanying Teacher's Resource Pack contains photocopiable materials for further practice and extra lessons, taking into consideration the needs of mixed-ability groups by providing extra material for fast finishers or students who need more support, as well as formal tests.

Student support: *English in Mind* offers systematic support to students through: Study help sections and Skills tips; classroom language; guidance in units to help with the development of classroom discourse and the students' writing; a wordlist including phonetic transcriptions and lists of irregular verbs and phonetics (at the back of the Student's Book); and a Grammar reference (at the back of the Workbook).

English in Mind: components

Each level of the *English in Mind* series contains the following components:

- Student's Book
- Class CDs or Class Cassettes
- Workbook with accompanying Audio CD / CD-ROM
- Teacher's Book
- Teacher's Resource Pack
- Website resources

The Student's Book

Modular structure: The *English in Mind* Student's Books are organised on a modular basis – each contains four modules of four units per module. The modules have broad themes and are organised as follows: a) a two-page module opener; b) four units of six pages each; c) a two-page Check your progress section.

Module openers are two pages which allow teachers to 'set the scene' for their students, concerning both the informational content and the language content of what is to come in the module itself. This helps both to motivate the students and to provide the important 'signposting' which allows them to see where their learning is going next. The pages contain: a) a visual task in which students match topics to a selection of photographs taken from the coming units; b) a list of skills learning objectives for the module; c) a short matching task which previews the main grammar content of the coming module; and d) a simple vocabulary task, again previewing the coming content.

The **units** have the basic following structure, although with occasional minor variations depending on the flow of an individual unit:

- an opening **reading** text
- a **grammar** page, often including pronunciation
- two pages of **vocabulary** and **skills** work
- either a **photo story** or a **Culture in mind** text, followed by **writing skills** work.

The **reading texts** aim to engage and motivate the students with interesting and relevant content, and to provide contextualised examples of target grammar and lexis. The texts have 'lead-in' tasks and are followed by comprehension tasks of various kinds. All the opening texts are also recorded on the Class CD/Cassette, which allows teachers to follow the initial reading with a 'read and listen' phase, giving the students the invaluable opportunity of connecting the written word with the spoken version, which is especially useful for auditory learners. Alternatively, with stronger classes, teachers may decide to do one of the exercises as a listening task, with books closed.

---

[3] See Marion Williams and Robert L. Burden: *Psychology for Language Teachers*, Cambridge University Press, 1997 (pp. 143–162), on how the learner deals with the process of learning.

Grammar follows the initial reading. The emphasis is on active involvement in the learning process. Examples from the texts are isolated and used as a basis for tasks, which focus on both concept and form of the target grammar area. Students are encouraged to find other examples and work out rules for themselves. Occasionally there are also Look boxes which highlight an important connected issue concerning the grammar area, for example, in Unit 1, work on adjectives has a Look box showing how the indefinite articles *a* and *an* are used. This is followed by a number of graded exercises, both receptive and productive, which allow students to begin to employ the target language in different contexts and to produce realistic language. Next, there is usually a speaking activity, aiming at further personalisation of the language.

Each unit has at least one **Vocabulary** section, with specific word fields. Again, examples from the initial text are focused on, and a lexical set is developed, with exercises for students to put the vocabulary into use. Vocabulary is frequently recycled in later texts in the unit (e.g. photo stories or Culture in mind texts), and also in later units.

Pronunciation is included in every unit. There are exercises on common phoneme problems such as /ð/ in *there* vs. /θ/ in *think*, as well as aspects of stress (within words, and across sentences) and elision.

Language skills are present in every unit. There is always at least one **listening skills** activity, with listening texts of various genres; at least one (but usually several) **speaking skills** activity for fluency development; **reading skills** are taught through the opening texts and also later texts in some units, as well as the Culture in mind sections. There is always a **writing skills** task, at the end of each unit.

The final two pages of each unit have either a **photo story** (odd-numbered units) or a **Culture in mind** text (even-numbered units). The **photo stories** are conversations between teenagers in everyday situations, allowing students to read and listen for interest and also to experience the use of common everyday language expressions. These Everyday English expressions are worked on in exercises following the dialogue. The **Culture in mind** texts are reading texts which provide further reading practice, and an opportunity for students to develop their knowledge and understanding of the world at large and in particular the English-speaking world. They include a wide variety of stimulating topics, for example, the popularity of pets in British homes, teenagers' television viewing habits, London's colourful Notting Hill carnival, the story of a South African hero and UK holiday camps – past and present.

The final activity in each unit is a **writing skills** task. These are an opportunity for students to further their control of language and to experiment in the production of tasks in a variety of genres (e.g. letters, emails, postcards, etc.). There are model texts for the students to aid their own writing, and exercises providing guidance in terms of content and organisation. Through the completion of the writing tasks, students, if they wish, can also build up a bank of materials, or 'portfolio', during their period of learning: this can be very useful to them as the source of a sense of clear progress and as a means of self-assessment. A 'portfolio' of work can also be shown to other people (exam bodies, parents, even future employers) as evidence of achievement in language learning. Many of the writing tasks also provide useful and relevant practice for examinations such as Cambridge ESOL KET or Trinity Integrated Skills Examinations.

When a module of four units closes, the module ends with a two-page **Check your progress** section. Here the teacher will find exercises in the Grammar, Vocabulary and Everyday English expressions that were presented in the module. The purpose of these (as opposed to the more formal tests offered in the Teacher's Resource Pack) is for teachers and students alike to check quickly the learning and progress made during the module just covered; they can be done in class or at home. Every exercise has a marking scheme, and students can use the marks they gain to do some simple self-assessment of their progress (a light 'task' is offered for this).

Beyond the modules and units themselves, *English in Mind* offers at the **end of the Student's Book** a further set of materials for teachers and students. These consist of:

- **Projects:** activities (one per module) which students can do in pairs or groups (or even individually if desired), for students to put the language they have so far learned into practical and enjoyable use. They are especially useful for mixed-ability classes, as they allow students to work at their own pace. The projects produced could also be part of the 'portfolio' of material mentioned earlier.
- An **irregular verb** list for students to refer to when they need.
- A listing of **phonetic symbols**, again for student reference.
- A **wordlist** with the core lexis of the Student's Book, with phonetic transcriptions. This is organised by unit, and within each unit heading there are the major word-fields, divided into parts of speech (verbs, nouns, adjectives, etc.). The wordlists are a feature that teachers can use in classrooms, for example, to develop students' reference skills, or to indicate ways in which they themselves might organise vocabulary notebooks, and by students at home, as a useful reference and also to prepare for tests or progress checks.

The Workbook

The Workbook is a resource for both teachers and students, providing further practice in the language and skills covered in the Student's Book. It is organised unit-by-unit, following the Student's Book. Each Workbook unit has six pages, and the following contents:

Remember and check: this initial exercise encourages students to remember the content of the initial reading text in the Student's Book unit.

Exercises: an extensive range of supporting exercises in the grammatical, lexical and phonological areas of the Student's Book unit, following the progression of the unit, so that teachers can use the exercises either during or at the end of the Student's Book unit.

Everyday English and **Culture in mind**: extra exercises on these sections in alternating units, as in the Student's Book.

Study help: these sections follow a syllabus of study skills areas, to develop the students' capacities as independent and successful learners. After a brief description of the skill, there are exercises for the students to begin to practise it.

Skills in mind page: these pages contain a separate skills development syllabus, which normally focuses on two main skill areas in each unit. There is also a skill tip relating to the main skill area, which the students can immediately put into action when doing the skills task(s).

Unit check page: this is a one-page check of knowledge of the key language of the unit, integrating both grammar and vocabulary in the three exercise types. The exercise types are: a) a cloze text to be completed using items given in a box; b) a sentence-level multiple choice exercise; c) a guided error correction exercise.

At the end of the Workbook, there is a **Grammar reference** section. Here, there are explanations of the main grammar topics of each unit, with examples. It can be used for reference by students at home, or the teacher might wish to refer to it in class if the students appreciate grammatical explanations.

The Workbook includes an **Audio CD / CD-ROM**, which contains both the listening material for the Workbook (listening texts and pronunciation exercises) and a CD-ROM element, containing definitions for the wordlist items with a spoken model for each one. A range of carefully graded grammar and vocabulary exercises provide further practice of language presented in each module.

The Teacher's Book

The Teacher's Book contains:

- clear, simple, practical teaching **notes** on each unit and how to implement the exercises as effectively as possible
- complete **tapescripts** for all listening and pronunciation activities
- complete **answers** to all exercises (grammar, vocabulary, comprehension questions, etc.)
- **optional further activities**, for stronger or weaker classes, to facilitate the use of the material in mixed-ability classes
- **background notes** relating to the information content (where appropriate) of reading texts and Culture in mind pages

- **language notes** relating to grammatical areas, to assist less-experienced teachers who might have concerns about the target language and how it operates (these can also be used to refer to the Workbook Grammar reference section)
- a complete **answer key** and **tapescripts** for the Workbook.

The Teacher's Resource Pack

This extra component, spiral bound for easy photocopying, contains the following photocopiable resources:

- an **Entry** test which can be used for diagnostic testing or also used for remedial work
- **module tests** containing separate sections for: Grammar, Vocabulary, Everyday English, Reading, Listening (the recordings for which are on the Class Cassettes/CDs), Speaking and Writing. A key for the Tests is also provided
- **photocopiable communicative activities**: one page for each unit reflecting the core grammar and/or vocabulary of the unit
- **photocopiable extra grammar exercises**: one page of four exercises for each unit, reflecting the key grammar areas of the unit
- **teaching notes** for the above.

Web resources

In addition to information about the series, the *English in Mind* website contains downloadable pages of further activities and exercises for students as well as other resources. It can be found at this part of the Cambridge University Press website:

www.cambridge.org/elt/englishinmind

Welcome!

Warm up

Ask students how old they think the characters in the photo are and what they think their names might be. Accept all answers at this stage.

1 Listen and read

Play the recording while students read and listen. Check their predictions from the *Warm up* at this point.

TAPESCRIPT
Hi! I'm Rob. What's your name?
I'm Amy, and this is Lucy.
Hello. My name's Alex.

> **Language note**
> You may want to explain to students that there are two ways of greeting people in English: Hello and Hi. Hello tends to be slightly more formal and used when people meet each other for the first time although both are acceptable.

2 Speak

Divide the class into small groups of three or four. Give students a few minutes to read through the gapped dialogue and check they understand that they must substitute their own names in the gaps. Ask a few stronger groups to read out their completed dialogues to the rest of the class.

Weaker classes: They may find it useful to read through Exercise 1 again before they start.

Module 1
Me and others

YOU WILL LEARN ABOUT ...

Ask students to look at the photos on the page. Ask them to read through the topics in the box and check they understand each item. You can ask them the following questions in L1 if appropriate: *Which city can you see? How do you say ... in English? Who is the writer in the photo? How many people are in your family?* In pairs or small groups, students discuss which topic area they think each photo matches. Check answers.

Answers
1   International words
2   Famous people
3   A famous writer
4   Countries and nationalities
5   British families

YOU WILL LEARN HOW TO ...

See Introduction.

Use grammar

Go through the first item with students. Stronger students should be able to continue with the other items on their own or in pairs.

Weaker classes: Put the grammar headings on the board and give an example of your own for each or encourage students to provide an example. In pairs, students now match the grammar items in their book. Check answers.

Answers
The verb *be*: Nick and Mike are 17.
Question words: Where are you from?
like / don't like: I don't like Ricky Martin.
Object pronouns: I really like them!
Present simple: He studies French at school.
Possessive *'s*: This is Peter's book.
Possessive adjectives: She's here in England with her family.

Use vocabulary

Write the headings on the board. Go through the items in the Student's Book and check understanding. Ask students if they can think of one more item for the *Classroom objects* heading, prompting them by picking up items from their desks if necessary. Add suggestions to the list on the board. Students now do the same for the other headings. Some possibilities are:

Classroom objects: *pen, ruler, paper, sharpener, rubber, notebook, desk, chair*

Adjectives: *big, cheap, old, young*

Nationalities: *Spanish, French, Portuguese, Russian, Brazilian, Mexican*

Family: *mother, father, brother, grandmother, grandfather, aunt, uncle*

1 I know!

1 Read and listen

Warm up

Books closed. Ask students if they can think of any words in English which are international words. Elicit suggestions and put them on the board.

(a) Students open their books at page 8 and read through the list of words. Check understanding and see if any students' predictions from the *Warm up* are in the list. Go through the first item as an example, if necessary. Students complete the exercise. Do not check answers at this stage.

(b) 🔊 Play the recording while students listen and check their answers to Exercise 1a. If your students are complete beginners you may need to translate the numbers on the recording. Play the recording a second time, pausing after each word for students to repeat. If students are having problems with some words, drill these as a class.

TAPESCRIPT

1 city 2 football 3 hamburger 4 hotel
5 museum 6 pizza 7 phone 8 restaurant
9 sandwich 10 taxi 11 TV 12 video

┌─ OPTIONAL ACTIVITY ─────────────

Weaker classes: Call out one of the numbers from the pictures on page 8 and a student's name. The student must name the object and use the correct pronunciation.

Stronger classes: Give students a few minutes to memorise the 12 pictures on page 8. Books closed. Call out the number of an object from page 8 and a student's name. The student must name the object correctly and use the correct pronunciation.

Vocabulary notebook
In their vocabulary notebooks, students can start a section called *International words*. They should note down any new words from this section and add any new words as they come across them.

2 Vocabulary
Classroom objects

(a) **Stronger classes:** Students look at the pictures on page 9. In pairs they can ask each other the example question and try to answer as many of the questions with the correct English word. If they are having problems, they can ask you the question. Remind students not to write anything down at this stage.

Weaker classes: Give students a few minutes to look at the pictures, then ask a student to demonstrate the question and then give them the answer. Remind students not to write anything down at this stage.

(b) 🔊 Students now read through the words in the box and write the correct words under the pictures in Exercise 2a. Give them a few minutes to complete the activity. Play the recording while students listen and check answers. If your students are complete beginners you may need to translate the numbers on the recording.

Play the recording a second time, pausing after each word for students to repeat.

TAPESCRIPT/ANSWERS

1 pen 2 book 3 board 4 cassette 5 pencil
6 chair 7 door 8 window 9 notebook
10 desk

Vocabulary notebook
In their vocabulary notebooks, students can start a section called *Classroom objects*. They should note down any new words from this section and add any new words as they come across them.

┌─ OPTIONAL ACTIVITY ─────────────

Collect up some small classroom objects (e.g. pen, pencil, notebook, cassette) and put them on a tray (a minimum of about 8 objects). Give students a few minutes to look at the tray and memorise the contents. Ask one student to come out and remove an object, while the others close their eyes. The students must then try and guess which object has been removed from the tray. The first person to get it right can come out and remove the next object.

3 Grammar

Plurals

Stronger classes: Students look at the pictures and identify each one. Remind them of the words they have just learnt in Exercise 2. Explain that there is more than one of each item in each picture so they must write the plural form of each noun. Go through the example as a class, asking a student to explain how the plural is formed (by adding an −s). Give students a few minutes to write their answers. Check answers as a class.

Weaker classes: Books closed. Ask students how many of the words they can remember from Exercise 2a and write them on the board. Explain to students that these are all singular words and ask them how they would form the plural of them. Elicit or explain that they would add an −s and ask a student to come out and add an −s to the words on the board to demonstrate how this works. Students now open their books at page 9 and write the plural forms of the nouns in the pictures in Exercise 3.

Check answers as a class, making sure students are using the correct pronunciation.

Answers

2 6 pencils   3 3 chairs   4 4 cassettes   5 5 books
6 6 notebooks

Look box

Students read through the information in the box. Explain that the words in the box are irregular plurals. Ask students if they know any other irregular plurals in English (e.g. child/children, foot/feet, tooth/teeth).

Language note

Explain to students that the plurals they have seen in this unit are regular (add −s) or irregular. There are other spelling rules for regular plurals which students may find it useful to know at this stage:

If a noun ends in −s, −z, −x, −ch, −sh: add −es (bus/buses).

If a noun ends in −y, change the −y to −i and add −es (baby/babies).

Exceptions to the rule are: potato/potatoes, tomato/tomatoes.

Grammar notebook

Students should note down the plural rules and some examples of their own in their grammar notebooks.

OPTIONAL ACTIVITY

Call out some singular nouns from this lesson or some others of your own and ask students to provide the correct plural form, asking them to spell them out if necessary.

4 Pronunciation

Word stress

a 🔊 Students read through the words in each column. Play the recording, pausing after each word for students to repeat. Ask students to explain the number of syllables in each column (A = 1 syllable, B = 2 syllables, C = 3 syllables). Remind them that they should repeat the words with the same stress as on the recording.

TAPESCRIPT

read   cheap   desk   open   teacher   hotel
computer   cinema   hamburger

b 🔊 Explain that students will hear some other words and they must listen and decide how many syllables are in each and then write them under the appropriate column. Do the first item with them as an example, if necessary. Students listen and write the words down under the appropriate column. Play the recording again for students to listen and check answers. Play the recording a third time, pausing after each word for students to repeat.

TAPESCRIPT

sandwich   door   museum   pen   restaurant
cassette

Answers

A: door, pen
B: sandwich, cassette
C: museum, restaurant

5 Vocabulary

Adjectives

a Students read through the words in the box. Check any problems. Ask a stronger student to explain what an adjective is (describes a noun). Ask students to point out the adjectives in the box. Go through the example as a class, making sure students understand what *cheap* means. Students complete the exercise. Do not check answers at this stage.

b 🔊 Play the recording for students to listen and check their answers.

TAPESCRIPT/ANSWERS

1 a cheap computer
2 an old man
3 an interesting film
4 a new book
5 a small hotel
6 a big TV
7 a bad singer
8 a good hamburger

(c) Ask students what they notice about the position of the adjectives in the phrases in Exercise 5a (the adjectives are all before the noun). Go through the example as a class then give students a few minutes to complete the exercise. Monitor and check students are putting the adjective in the correct position. Check answers.

Answers
2 a good CD
3 an expensive restaurant
4 an interesting museum
5 a good football team
6 an interesting computer game

Language note
It may be useful to point out to students at this stage that adjectives in English do not change with the noun, the adjective stays the same whether the noun is singular or plural. We say: *A good book / three good books* NOT ~~three goods books~~.

Look box
Students read through the examples in the box. Ask them what the difference is between the first two examples and the second two examples (the first two have *a* because the adjective begins with a consonant and the second two have *an* because the adjective begins with a vowel). If students need further practice with this, give them a few examples of your own.

(d) Go through the example as a class and then in pairs students can provide an example for each item in Exercise 5b. Ask pairs to read out their examples to the rest of the class.

(e) Students read through the list of adjectives. Go through the example as a class. Students complete the exercise. Check answers.

Answers
big – small
boring – interesting
old – new
cheap – expensive

┌─ OPTIONAL ACTIVITY ─────────────────
Ask students to provide an example of their own for the adjectives in Exercise 5e.

Vocabulary notebook
Remind students to note down the adjectives from this section in their notebooks.

6 Listen

(a) 🔊 Play the recording for students to listen. Play the recording a second time, pausing after each letter for students to repeat.

TAPESCRIPT
A B C D E F G H I J K L M N O P Q R S T U V W X Y Z

(b) Write the sounds of the alphabet on the board. Go through each sound as a class, making sure students can hear the sound clearly.

Stronger classes: They can classify the remaining letters. Do not check answers at this stage.

Weaker classes: It may be helpful to go through each sound individually with them, replaying the recording from Exercise 6a for them to listen again. Do not check answers at this stage.

(c) 🔊 Play the recording for students to listen and check their answers.

TAPESCRIPT/ANSWERS
/e/   f, l, m, n, s, x, z
/eɪ/   a, h, j, k
/iː/   b, c, d, e, g, p, t, v
/aɪ/   i, y
/əʊ/   o
/uː/   q, u, w
/ɑː/   r

(d) Go through the example as a class. Point out to students that we can also say 'double ...' in English when there are two letters the same in a word. In pairs, students think of names and spell them out to their partner, who must work out if the spelling is correct.

┌─ OPTIONAL ACTIVITY ─────────────────
Make up various bingo cards using the letters of the alphabet. Copy and give these out to students. Call out the letters of the alphabet in a random order (keeping a note of the letters you have called out). The first student to cross off all the letters on their card and to call out *Bingo!* is the winner.

Alternatively, this can be done as a small group or pair activity.

7 Vocabulary
Numbers 0–20

(a) 🔊 Books closed. Elicit as many numbers from 0 to 20 as students know and write them on the board (or ask students to come out and write them up if time permits). Students open their books at page 11 and quickly read through the numbers. Play the recording, pausing after each number for students to repeat.

TAPESCRIPT
zero one two three four five six seven eight nine ten eleven twelve thirteen fourteen fifteen sixteen seventeen eighteen nineteen twenty

b Prepare a list of numbers between one and twenty to read to the class, pausing after the first item to go through as an example, if necessary. Read the rest of the list for students to listen and tick the numbers they hear. Check answers, reading your list of numbers again as necessary.

c 🔊 Explain to students that they will hear a few phone numbers on the recording. It may be useful to explain to them (or elicit) that in English we say phone numbers in two ways, e.g. 712345 = seven one two/three four five or seven one/two three/four five. Also explain to students that where there are two numbers the same we say 'double ...'. Play the recording, pausing after the first phone number, if necessary. Play the rest of the recording while students listen and write down the numbers they hear.

TAPESCRIPT/ANSWERS
1 My phone number is 272 3454. That's 272 3454.
2 My phone number is 681 7595. Once more: 681 7595.
3 Hi John? It's Tom. Phone me, can you? It's 923 6931. OK? 923 6931.
4 Hi. This is 717 4930. Please leave a message after the tone.

d Divide the class into pairs. Ask a stronger pair to demonstrate the example question and answer. Give students a few minutes to ask and answer.

┌─ OPTIONAL ACTIVITY ──────────
You can give students some simple sums using the numbers 0 to 20.

Numbers 20–100

e 🔊 Books closed. Elicit as many numbers between 20 and 100 as students know and write them on the board. Students open their books at page 11 and quickly read through the numbers. Play the recording, pausing after each number for students to repeat.

TAPESCRIPT
twenty   thirty   forty   fifty   sixty   seventy   eighty   ninety   a hundred

f Students read through the numbers. Ask them how to pronounce them. Play the recording for students to listen and check their pronunciation. Pause the recording after each number for students to repeat.

TAPESCRIPT
1 twenty-six   2 twenty-nine   3 thirty-five   4 forty-seven   5 fifty-eight   6 sixty-four

Vocabulary notebook
Remind students to make a note of all the numbers from this section in their notebooks.

┌─ OPTIONAL ACTIVITY ──────────
Give students the following extra exercise for practice in distinguishing between -*teen* numbers and -*ty* numbers. Write the following on the board:
1   13 or 30?
2   90 or 19?
3   18 or 80?
4   50 or 15?
5   17 or 70?

Choose which number you are going to call out, making a note of it each time and then ask students to read out their answers.

Alternatively, you can give them some more sums using all the numbers from 0 to 100.

No problem

8 Read and listen

Warm up

Give students a few minutes to look at the photo story and ask them the following questions: *What are the characters' names? (Rob, Amy and Lucy) Where are they? (In a Maths class) What is the woman's job? (She is a Maths teacher).* Accept all suggestions at this stage but do not offer the correct answers.

a 🔊 Play the recording while students read and listen to the story. Check their predictions to the *Warm up.* Play the recording again, pausing as necessary for students to clarify any problems.

TAPESCRIPT
See the photo story on page 12 of the Student's Book.

b Students look at the pictures and the names and match them. Go through the first one as an example, if necessary. Check answers.

Answers
Rob   Amy   Lucy

┌─ OPTIONAL ACTIVITY ──────────
In small groups, students can act out the photo story dialogue.

9 Everyday English

(a) Students read through the words. Check any problems. Go through the example as a class making sure students understand they must match the words on the left with words on the right to make sentences from the photo story.

Weaker classes: Students may find it helpful to read the photo story again before completing this exercise.

Check answers.

Answers
What's the answer?
I don't understand.
No problem.
That's right.

(b) Divide the class into pairs. Give students a few minutes to read through items 1 to 8. Go through the first item as a class, asking students how they would express this in their own language. Remind them that there may not be an exact translation. Pairs can compare answers before a whole class check. Discuss any different translations as a class.

10 Listen and write

(a) 🔊 Ask students: *Who is the first message to (Lucy) and who is it from (Mrs Hurley)?* Students quickly read through the message. Play the recording while students read the text again. Check answers.

TAPESCRIPT
Hello, this is Mrs Hurley with a message for Lucy. The homework is on page 78. If there are any problems, my number is 01433 651464. Bye now.

(b) 🔊 Students read the gapped message. Ask them what information is missing (person's name, page number and telephone number). Students listen to the recording and complete the missing information.

Weaker classes: They may find it helpful to listen to the whole message first, then it can be played and paused after each gap.

Check answers.

TAPESCRIPT/ANSWERS

Girl   Hello?

Woman   Hello, it's Mrs Booker. Is Rob there please?

Girl   No sorry. Can I take a message?

Woman   Oh yes please. My name is Mrs Booker, that's B double O K E R, I'm Rob's English teacher. Please tell him the homework is on page 85.

Girl   Page 85. OK!

Woman   And my phone number is 01763 208956.

Girl   01763. Er...

Woman   208956. Thanks very much.

Girl   OK. Bye Mrs Booker.

Woman   Goodbye.

② She isn't American

TOPIC: Countries and nationalities

TEXTS
Reading and listening: a game show quiz
Reading and listening: *Culture in mind: Heroes and heroines*
Writing: information about yourself

SPEAKING
Talking about nationalities and where people are from

LANGUAGE
Grammar: The verb *be* (singular): statements and questions; Question words: *who, what, how old, where?*
Vocabulary: Countries and nationalities

1 Read and listen

Warm up

Give students a few minutes to look at the pictures. Ask them: *What is happening? (A game show quiz) Where is this taking place? (On television) What are the contestants' names? (Carol and Jonathan).* Accept all suggestions at this point but do not give the answers.

(a) 🔊 Students read the question. Play the recording while students listen and read. Check answers and check their answers to the *Warm up*.

TAPESCRIPT

See the dialogue on page 14 of the Student's Book.

Answer
Carol

(b) 🔊 Give students a few minutes to look at the pictures and names of the stars in the box. Tell them that they must match the names to the pictures. Play the recording, pausing to give students time to write the names in the spaces. Students can compare answers in pairs before checking as a class.

TAPESCRIPT/ANSWERS

Host   And now for round two of the show, *Who's the star?* This round is for our viewers at home. Look at the four pictures of stars. Who are they? Now listen carefully. Jonathan?

Jonathan   OK. Number one's a tennis player. She's Belgian. Er ... Kim Clijsters?

Host   Thanks very much, Jonathan. Six points for you. And now it's your turn, Carol.

Carol   OK. Number two's famous. OK. ... It's the singer Ricky Martin.

Host   Excellent, Carol! Six points for you too. And now Jonathan's turn. Who's number three?

Jonathan   OK ... . This is easy. She's the famous singer and actress Jennifer Lopez.

Host   Well done, Jonathan! Another six points for you. Now Carol. Who's number four?

Carol   Number four is Italian, and he's a singer. He's very famous. And he is of course ... Luciano Pavarotti.

Host   Excellent, Carol! Six points for you. So we have a tie-break! And now for the winner of those of you at home. Hello? Who's this? Hello Larry, this is...

OPTIONAL ACTIVITY

In pairs or small groups, students think of a famous person of their choice. The other student(s) take turns to ask a maximum of five questions and the person who has thought of the character can only answer Yes or No. If the students have not guessed the character after five guesses the person can give them the answer and have another turn. The student who guesses correctly has a turn with a new character. Points can be given to make this more interesting: five points for guessing after one question, four after two etc.

2 Grammar

The verb *be* (singular)

(a) **Stronger classes:** Students look at the sentences. Ask them which sentences are positive, negative and questions. Ask them what they notice about the verb in each one (positive: I'm, you're), negative (uses n't), question (subject and verb inverted). This can be done in L1 if necessary.

Weaker classes: Books closed. Write some example sentences of your own on the board, e.g. *I'm XXX., Am I a teacher?, You're a student., I'm not a singer.* Ask students what they notice about the verb in each sentence and elicit the positive, negative and question forms. Students now open their books at page 15 and look at the examples from the quiz show. Ask them which person each verb is for (I'm = first person, Is she = third person, You're = second person, She isn't = third person) and then ask them to identify the different forms.

(b) Students read through the table quickly and fill in the missing verbs. Give them a few minutes to do this, reminding them to refer back to the quiz show examples to help them. Check answers.

Answers
Positive: You're, She's, It's
Negative: She isn't, It isn't
Question: Are, Is, Is, Is
Short answer: are, aren't, is, is, isn't, is, isn't

Language note
Remind students that we use the word *not* to make a positive verb negative. If you feel it would be useful for students, explain that the short form is usually used when speaking and the full form when writing more formally.

OPTIONAL ACTIVITY
If you want to check students' understanding of the form at this point, call out a verb form and the person and then a student's name. The student must supply you with the correct verb form and the correct person.

c This exercise can be set for homework. Students read through sentences 1 to 4. Go through the first item as an example, if necessary. Students complete the exercise. Check answers.

Answers
1 'm   2 's   3 're   4 's

d This exercise can be set for homework. Students read through sentences 1 to 4. Go through the example as a class, if necessary. Students complete the exercise. Remind students they are using the negative form this time. Check answers.

Answers
2   She isn't a film star.
3   You're not the winner.
4   I'm not a tennis player.

Look box
Students read the examples in the box. Ask them what they notice about the positive and the question form in English (to make the question form we invert the subject and the verb).

e This exercise can be set for homework. Students read through questions 1 to 4. Go through the first item as an example. Students complete the exercise. Remind them to look carefully at the subject of each sentence before they choose the verb. Check answers.

Answers
1 Am   2 Are   3 Is   4 Is

f Divide the class into pairs. Ask a stronger pair to demonstrate the example question and answer. Give students a few minutes to ask and answer and then ask a few pairs to feedback to the class.

Language note
Explain to students that in English we use the verb *be* when asking about someone's age. We say: *I am 15.* NOT ~~I have 15 years~~.

Grammar notebook
Remind students to note down the verb forms from this unit in their notebooks.

3 Vocabulary
Countries
Warm up

Books closed. Ask students how many countries they know the names of in English. Elicit the names and put them on the board. Check the pronunciation of each country they have given.

Alternatively, you could use a large wall map and ask students to come out and identify the countries they know the names of in English.

a ◁))) Give students a few minutes to read through the names of the countries. Play the recording, pausing after each country for students to repeat. Point out the stress marks above each country and if students have produced countries in the *Warm up* which are not in this exercise, ask them to identify the number of syllables in each country.

TAPESCRIPT
Spain   Belgium   Britain   Poland   Brazil   Switzerland

b ◁))) Give students a few minutes to read through the countries in the box.

Stronger classes: They can pronounce the countries themselves and decide on the number of syllables and fit them into the table. They can listen and check only.

Weaker classes: Play the recording once for students to listen only. Play the recording a second time, pausing to give students time to fill in the table.

TAPESCRIPT
China   Russia   Turkey   Japan   Italy
Canada   Germany   `

Answers
Column 1: Russia, Turkey
Column 2: Japan
Column 3: Italy, Canada, Germany

c Divide the class into pairs. Give students a few minutes to look at the map. Ask a stronger pair to demonstrate the example question and answer. Students complete the exercise. Students can compare answers with another pair but do not check answers at this stage.

d ◁))) Play the recording for students to listen and check their answers to Exercise 3c.

TAPESCRIPT/ANSWERS
1 Canada   2 Brazil   3 Britain   4 Belgium
5 Germany   6 Spain   7 Switzerland   8 Italy
9 Poland   10 Turkey   11 Russia   12 China
13 Japan

e Give students a few minutes to look at the photos. Go through the example as a class.

Answers
1 Italy   2 Japan   3 Britain
4 Brazil   5 Poland   6 Turkey

OPTIONAL ACTIVITY

You will need a large wall map.

Whole class or small groups. Point to a country and ask a student to name it in English and then spell the name out. The student who answers correctly can come out and choose another country. You can award points for each correct country and spelling.

Vocabulary notebook
Encourage students to start a section called *Countries* in their vocabulary notebooks and to note down the countries from this section and any others they come across later in the course.

4 Grammar

Where are you from?

Warm up

Give students a few minutes to look at the pictures and read the dialogues. Can students predict where the children are from? Accept all suggestions at this stage but do not give the answers.

a 🔊 Play the recording while students listen and complete the dialogues and check their predictions from the *Warm up*.

Weaker classes: Play the recording once and then play it a second time, pausing after each gap to give them time to fill in the answers.

Check answers.

TAPESCRIPT/ANSWERS

Andrea   Hi! I'm Andrea. I'm from Switzerland.

Tomasz   Hi, Andrea. I'm Tomasz.

Andrea   Where are you from, Tomasz?

Tomasz   Poland.

OPTIONAL ACTIVITY

Weaker classes
In pairs, students can act out the dialogue from Exercise 4a.

Stronger classes
In pairs, they can invent new information and identities for themselves and then act out the dialogue from Exercise 4a.

b Students read through items 1 to 3. Students complete the exercise. Check answers.

Answers
1 'm   2 are   3 from

Grammar notebook
Remind students to note down the new structures from this section in their notebooks.

5 Pronunciation

from

a 🔊 Play the recording and see if students can hear the different ways *from* is pronounced.

TAPESCRIPT

Andrea   I'm from Switzerland.

Andrea   Where are you from?

b 🔊 Play the recording again, pausing for students to repeat each sentence. If students are having problems with the pronunciation, give them a few more examples of your own to drill as a class.

6 Vocabulary

Nationalities

Warm up

Write the countries from Exercise 3b on the board. Ask students if they know or can work out the nationality adjectives for any of them. Students can come out and write the nationalities they know beside the relevant country if there is time.

a Give students a few minutes to read through the countries in the box. Go through the examples as a class, making sure students can see which endings go in which column. Students complete the exercise. They can then add in any other countries from the *Warm up* to the table. Do not check answers at this stage.

b 🔊 Play the recording while students check their answers. Alternatively, write the column headings on the board and ask students to come and write the nationalities under the correct heading. Check spelling. Play the recording a second time, pausing after each adjective for students to repeat. Make sure students are using the correct stress when pronouncing the nationality adjectives.

Italian   Canadian   Belgian   Brazilian   Russian
Polish   British   Turkish   Spanish
Chinese   Japanese   Portuguese

Answers
Column 1: Brazilian, Belgian, Russian, Canadian
Column 2: Turkish, British, Spanish
Column 3: Japanese, Portuguese

(c) Give students a few minutes to look at the flags and read through the nationalities. Go through the first item as an example, if necessary. Students complete the exercise. Do not check answers at this stage.

(d) Divide the class into pairs. Ask a stronger pair to demonstrate the example. Give students a few minutes to discuss their answers to Exercise 6c.

(e) 🔊 Play the recording for students to check answers.

TAPESCRIPT/ANSWERS
1 Belgian   2 Chinese   3 Polish   4 Russian
5 Turkish   6 Italian   7 British   8 Brazilian

Look box
Students read through the examples in the box. Elicit the rule for nationality adjectives which start with a vowel and a consonant. Students may remember this rule from Unit 1 and the use of adjectives.

Vocabulary notebook
Encourage students to start a section called *Nationalities* and to note down the nationalities from this section.

┌─ OPTIONAL ACTIVITY ─────────────
│ Small groups. Students take turns to choose a famous
│ person and the other students must guess who the
│ person is. The person who has chosen must give
│ information to the rest of the group. For example:
│
│ *S1: I am from [country]. I am not American. I am a film
│ star.*
│
│ The student who guesses correctly takes the next turn
│ and so on.

7 Grammar

wh- question words

(a) Students read through the question words. Elicit how they say them in their own language. Ask them if they know which words apply to the following things: people (who), places (where), things (what) and manner (how) and elicit the answers.

(b) Students read through items 1 to 6. Go through the example as a class, asking students what they notice about these questions (the verb goes immediately after the question word). Students complete the exercise. Check answers.

Answers
2 Where   3 What   4 Where   5 How   6 Who

┌───────────────────────────────────
│ **Language note**
│ Draw students' attention to the full and short
│ forms following question words and explain that
│ in English we only use the short form of the third
│ person singular after question words and we
│ cannot shorten the other forms. We say: *Where's
│ the …?* NOT ~~*Where're the …?*~~

Grammar notebook
Encourage students to start a section called *wh-*question words and to note down the question words and some examples of their own.

Heroes and heroines

8 Speak

If you set the background information as a homework research task, ask students to tell the rest of the class what they found out.

BACKGROUND INFORMATION

Pierce Brosnan: Was born in 1953 in Ireland. Brosnan made his first James Bond film in 1995, *Goldeneye*. He went on to make *Tomorrow Never Dies* in 1997, *The World is Not Enough* in 1999 and *Die Another Day* in 2002.

Zinedine Zidane (Zizou): Was born on 26th June 1972 in Marseille, France, the son of Algerian immigrants. He started his career as a soccer player with the US club, Saint-Henri. He played professional football in Cannes, Bordeaux and Juventus. In 2001, he made football history when he was transferred to Real Madrid for £46 million. He is also Christian Dior's first male model.

Venus Williams: Venus was born on 17th June 1980 in Lynwood California. Coached by their father, Venus and her sister Serena took the tennis world by storm in the late 1990s. Serena beat Venus in 2002 in the French and US Opens and at Wimbledon.

Alicia Keys: Was born Alicia Augello Cook on January 4th 1981 in New York. She signed a deal with Arista Records in 1998. Her music is said to be a mixture of pop, Gospel, R & B and soul and her debut album was released in 2001, *Songs in a Minor*.

Gisele Bundchen: Was born Gisele Caroline Bundchen on July 20th 1980 in Horizontina, Rio Grande do Sul, Brazil. She was discovered eating a meal in a fast food restaurant in Sao Paolo at the age of 14. Since then she has worked for many major fashion houses including Ralph Lauren, Dolce and Gabbana and Versace.

Enrique Iglesias: Was born in Madrid on May 8th 1975. He is the son of the singer Julio Iglesias and the model Isabel Preysler. He enjoys international success as a singer and songwriter with his songs recorded in four languages: Spanish, Portuguese, Italian and English.

Annika Sorenstam: Was born on October 9th 1970 in Stockholm, Sweden. Her parents were both sports enthusiasts and Annika grew up with tennis as her first passion. She moved to London at the age of ten still playing tennis and it was not until her early teens that she discovered her talent for golf. At the age of 19 she went to the University of Arizona to study and she won several golf titles. In 2002 she excelled, winning 11 titles in the international golfing arena.

Warm up

Ask students if they know any of the famous people in the pictures and where they come from.

Divide the class into pairs. Give students a few minutes to read through the information and check any problems. Go through the example sentence as a class, drawing students' attention to the use of the third person singular *be* form. Students complete the exercise. Remind students that they may not always be able to use the short form after the name of the person. Monitor and check students are using the third person singular forms correctly, noting down any repeated errors to go through as a class after the exercise. Do not check answers at this stage.

Answers
2   Gisele Bundchen's a model. She's from Horizontina. She's Brazilian.
3   Alicia Keys is a singer. She's from New York. She's American.
4   Venus Williams is a tennis player. She's from California. She's American.
5   Enrique Iglesias is a singer. He's from Madrid. He's Spanish.
6   Pierce Brosnan's an actor. He's from Navan. He's Irish.
7   Annika Sorenstam's a golfer. She's from Stockholm. She's Swedish.

9 Listen

(a) ◁)) Play the recording for students to listen and check their answers.

TAPESCRIPT/ANSWERS
1   My hero is a football player from Marseille in France. His name is Zinedine Zidane.

2   My heroine is a model. Her name is Gisele Bundchen. She's Brazilian. She's from Horizontina.
3   My heroine is a singer. She's from New York in the USA. Her name is Alicia Keys.
4   My heroine is from California in the States. She's a tennis player. Her name is Venus Williams.
5   My hero is a singer. He's from Madrid, in Spain. He's Enrique Iglesias.
6   My hero is Irish. He's from Navan, County Meath and he's an actor. Of course, it's Pierce Brosnan.
7   Annika Sorenstam is my heroine. She's a golfer from Stockholm in Sweden.

(b) Students read through sentences 1 to 7. Go through the example as a class, reminding students that they must correct the information if it is false. Remind them to use their answers from Exercise 9a to help them. Students complete the exercise. Check answers.

Answers
2   No, she isn't. She's from California.
3   No, she isn't. She's from New York.
4   No, he isn't. He's Spanish.
5   No, he isn't. He's a footballer.
6   No, she isn't. She's from Horizontina.
7   No, she isn't. She's from Sweden.

(c) In pairs, students discuss who their hero or heroine is. They must say where the person is from and what they do. Ask pairs to feedback to the rest of the class about their partner. Monitor and check students are using the correct question and answer forms: *Who is your hero/heroine? Where is he/she from?* etc. and note down any repeated errors to go through as a class after the exercise.

10 Writing
Warm up

(a) Give students a few minutes to read the example text and answer the questions.

(b) This part of the writing can be set for homework. Encourage students to make notes on the areas the text covers: name, age, nationality, where from, address, phone number, hero/heroine and where hero/heroine is from. Students can then draft their notes before checking them and writing the full text.

┌─ OPTIONAL ACTIVITY ─────────────
Students can expand the writing activity and add a photo of themselves and their hero/heroine.

③ We're a new band

1 Read and listen

Warm up

Ask students which bands or pop singers they enjoy listening to. Ask them if they can tell the rest of the class the country the singer/group comes from and their nationality.

(a) Discuss these questions as a class or in small groups. Ask groups to feedback. Are there any interesting results? Is there a band/singer which most students prefer?

(b) (◁») Students read through the two questions. Play the recording while students read and listen. Check answers. Play the recording a second time, pausing after each answer if necessary.

Weaker classes: Ask students to predict the kind of information they are likely to need to listen for in each answer.

TAPESCRIPT
See reading text on page 20 of the Student's Book.

Answers
1 Four
2 Nick is from Cambridge and the other members are from London.

(c) Students read through statements 1 to 5. Check any problems. Go through the first item as an example, if necessary.

Stronger classes: They can answer the questions without reading or listening again and can read and listen to check only. They can then correct the false answers.

Weaker classes: Play the recording while they read the interview again before they answer the questions.

Check answers. Play the recording again, pausing after each answer.

Answers
1 False. Nick is the singer, Zoe is the interviewer.
2 False. Nick is from Cambridge and the other members are from London.
3 False. Nick is 17, Mike is 19.
4 True
5 True

2 Grammar

The verb *be*: plural, negatives and questions

(a) **Stronger classes:** Students read through the three examples. Ask them to identify the positive, negative and question forms. Then ask them to provide an example of their own for each form. Ask them what they notice about the difference between the three forms.

Weaker classes: Books closed. Write the following examples (or some of your own) on the board: *We're in an English class. / We aren't (nationality). / Are you from (country)?* Ask students to identify the positive, negative and question forms. Students open their books at page 21 and read through the examples. Ask them what they notice about the difference between the three forms.

> **Language note**
> Remind students that we use *not* in the negative form of the verb *be* and that in English we invert the subject and the verb in questions. For example, we say: *Are you …?* NOT ~~You are…?~~

(b) Students read through the gapped table. Go through the first item with them as an example. Remind them these are the plural forms they are completing. Students complete the exercise. Check answers.

Answers
Positive: 're, 're
Negative: aren't, aren't
Question: Are, Are
Short answers: are/aren't, are/aren't, are/aren't

To check understanding of the plural forms at this point you may want to call out a person and a form and then ask a student to give you the form you are looking for.

c Students read through items 1 to 3. Go through the example, making sure students remember they are practising the plural forms. Students complete the exercise. Check answers.

Answers
1 aren't; 're
2 Are; aren't
3 Are; aren't; 're

d This exercise can be set for homework. Students read through items 1 to 4. Go through the example as a class, making sure students are aware that they are practising singular and plural forms. Elicit the singular forms quickly, if necessary before they start. Students complete the exercise. Check answers.

Answers
2 it isn't
3 Are; they're
4 Are; they aren't

e This exercise can be set for homework. Students read through questions 1 to 6 and look at the pictures. Go through the example as a class, drawing students' attention to the use of the third person singular question form. Remind them that they may also need to use the plural question form. Students complete the exercise. Check answers.

Answers
2 Are   3 Is   4 Are   5 Is   6 Is

┌─ OPTIONAL ACTIVITY ─────────────────

Weaker classes: In pairs, students answer the questions from Exercise 2e using the appropriate short answer.

Stronger classes: They can answer the questions from Exercise 2e and then write some more questions of their own for their partner to answer.
└

3 Vocabulary
Positive and negative adjectives

a Write the headings 'Very good' and 'Very bad' on the board. Students read the words in the box. Ask volunteers to come out and classify the words in the box under the relevant headings. Then ask students to give an example of their own for each adjective.

Weaker classes: Write the headings on the board but then put each adjective into a sentence of your own and ask students to classify each adjective.

Answers
Very good: fantastic, wonderful, great
Very bad: awful, terrible

┌──────────────────────────────────────┐
Language note: Remind students that in English adjectives go before the noun and that they do not change if the noun is singular or plural.
└──────────────────────────────────────┘

b Divide the class into pairs. Students read through the words in the box. Check any problems. Go through the example as a class, if necessary. Give students a few minutes to decide on their examples. Monitor and check students are using the example phrase correctly and that they are using the adjectives correctly. Ask pairs to feedback to the class. Are there any interesting answers? If so, ask students to give more information.

┌─ OPTIONAL ACTIVITY ─────────────────

Weaker classes: Books closed. Call out an adjective from the box in Exercise 3a. Ask a student to give you its opposite. That student can then call out another adjective from the box and ask another student to give the opposite.

Stronger classes: You can do this with other adjectives if students know more.
└

4 Grammar and speaking
I (don't) like ... / Do you like ...?

a **Stronger classes:** Students read through the phrases in the box and look at the faces. Give them a few minutes to classify each phrase under the appropriate face. Ask students to identify which is the positive and which is the negative form. Students can give you an example of their own using each expression.

Weaker classes: Books closed. Give students an example of your own using I like / I don't like. Ask students to identify which is the positive and which is the negative form. Students open their books at page 22. Follow the procedure for Stronger classes.

b Students read through the sentences. Give them a few minutes to write their answers. Students then read through the examples in the grammar table. Ask them what they notice about the questions and short answer forms (they both use the auxiliary do/don't).

┌──────────────────────────────────────┐
Language note
Students may produce statements like ~~I like swim~~. Remind them that in English we always use the –ing form after like / don't like.
└──────────────────────────────────────┘

c Divide the class into pairs. Students take turns to tell their partner their answers to the items in Exercise 4b. Monitor and check students are using the verb like correctly, making a note of any repeated errors to go through as a class after the exercise.

d Students can work with the same partner as they did in Exercise 4c or they can work with a different partner. Students read through the box and look at the illustrations. Check any problems. Ask a stronger pair to demonstrate the example dialogue, drawing students' attention to the use of the question and short answer forms and the positive and negative adjectives from Exercise 3. Give students a few minutes to ask and answer about the items in the box. Monitor and check students are asking and answering using the correct forms and make a note of any repeated errors to go through as a class after the exercise. Ask pairs to feedback to the rest of the class.

5 Grammar
Object pronouns

a 🔊 Ask students if A likes Madonna (No, he/she doesn't). Play the recording while students read and listen. Check answers.

Then ask students who *him* and *her* refer to in the dialogue and elicit Robbie Williams and Madonna. Explain that these words are object pronouns and are used to refer to someone or something which has already been mentioned.

TAPESCRIPT
See dialogue on page 23 of the Student's Book.

b **Stronger classes:** Students read through the words in the box. Explain that these are all the object pronouns. Go through the example, if necessary. Students complete the table.

Weaker classes: Write the headings *Subject pronouns* and *Object pronouns* on the board and ask a student to come and fill in the example items from Exercise 5a. Draw students' attention to the change from *he* to *him* and *she* to *her*. Follow the procedure for Stronger classes.

Check answers.

Answers
Object: me, her, him, it, us, them

To check understanding at this point, call out a subject pronoun and a student's name. The student must give the correct object pronoun.

c This exercise can be set for homework. Students read through items 1 to 4. Do the first item as an example, if necessary. Students complete the exercise. Remind students to look carefully at the subject of each sentence before they decide which object pronoun to choose. Check answers.

Answers
1 him   2 them   3 her   4 us

6 Pronunciation
/ɪ/ and /iː/

a 🔊 Play the recording while students listen to the pronunciation of each word.

TAPESCRIPT
big   three

b **Stronger classes:** Students read through the list of words. Do the first item as an example, showing them how to classify the word according to its pronunciation.

Students complete the exercise. Do not check answers at this stage.

Weaker classes: Write the headings on the board. Check students can hear the difference in the two words, playing the recording for Exercise 6a again if necessary. Give students a few minutes to read through the words in the box. Go through the first word as an example, asking a student to come out and write it under the correct heading. Continue like this until students have classified all the words under the headings on the board.

c 🔊 Play the recording, pausing after each word for students to check their answers.

Weaker classes: If there are still problems, play the recording again, pausing for students to repeat each word.

TAPESCRIPT/ANSWERS
/ɪ/: six, it, city, video
/iː/: he, we, cheap, fourteen

┌─ **OPTIONAL ACTIVITY** ─────────────
In small groups, give students a few minutes to see if they can think of any more words to add to each group.

Example answers
/ɪ/: Britney, thirty
/iː/: tree, see, me, thirteen

7 Listen and speak

BACKGROUND INFORMATION

U2: They are a popular Irish band from the 1980s who are still producing hit singles today. Their lead singer Bono is famous for his tireless campaigns to drop the third world debt and he regularly meets with world famous political leaders.

Manchester United: Is a very successful football club from the north west of England. They have had many famous managers over the years, including Sir Alex Ferguson. They have won the English League several times as well as a number of European competitions over the years. Famous players include Ruud Van Nistelroy, David Beckham, Roy Keane.

Tom Cruise: Was born on July 3rd, 1962 in Syracuse, New York. He started his acting career on stage despite problems with dyslexia. He made his name in 1983 in the film *The Outsiders*. His career flourished in 1988 with the release of *Top Gun* and other films he has made include *Rain Man* (1988) and *Born on the*

Fourth of July (1989). In 1987 he married the actress Mimi Rogers but they divorced in 1990. In 1990, after a whirlwind romance with Nicole Kidman, whom he met on the set of *Days of Thunder*, the couple married. They divorced in August 2001.

Christina Aguilera: Was born on December 18th, 1980, on Staten Island, New York. When she was 12, she got a part in the Mickey Mouse Club and became a Mouseketeer working with now-famous co-stars like Britney Spears and Justin Timberlake. Her first record deal was when she was 15 and she won a Grammy for Best New Artist. Her first album, *Christina Aguilera*, included the hits *Genie in a Bottle*, *Come on Over* and *What a Girl Wants*. She also had a hit with *P!nk*.

Pelé: Was born Edson Arantes do Nascimento in Brazil in 1940. His father had played as a professional footballer in the Brazilian league. Pelé played for amateur sides until he went to Santos football club, aged 15. He enjoyed massive success for his club throughout his career. He made his debut for the Brazilian national team in 1957, aged 16. The next year he played in his first World Cup, and showed the world his repertoire of amazing skills. He scored twice in the final, and Brazil was crowned champions. In the 1970s Pele played for the New York Cosmos.

Salma Hayek: Was born on September 2, 1966, in Coatzacoalcos, Veracruz. She went to college in Mexico City but pursued an acting career. Salma got jobs in television commercials, which led to a part in a daytime TV show. Selma was then cast as the title character in a popular soap, *Theresa*. Salma's popularity grew quickly and soon she was the best-known actress in Mexico. She moved to Los Angeles in 1991 and got her big break two years later with the lead part in *Desperado*.

a 🔊 Give students a few minutes to look at the pictures. Check any pronunciation problems, if necessary. Explain that students will hear four people talking about the people or things in the pictures. Play the recording while students listen.

Stronger classes: Explain that students must now complete the table with information from the recording. They can complete the table and then listen and check only.

Weaker classes: Play the recording again for students to listen only. Then play the first part of the recording again, pausing after Speaker 1 to give students time to complete this part of the table.

Continue in this way until students have completed the table. Check answers, playing and pausing the recording again as necessary.

TAPESCRIPT
1 I love football and I really like Manchester United. I think they're a great team.
2 I really like music and especially good singers. I like Bono and U2 a lot. I think they're fantastic. I also like Alicia Keys, but the one singer I don't like is Christina Aguilera.
3 I like music, and I like football. Oh, er, and I really like Pelé, you know, the Brazilian football player. He's my favourite.
4 I think Salma Hayek is fantastic. I love all her films. Er ... oh, and I think Tom Cruise is a good actor but I don't like him.

Answers
Speaker 1 Like: football, Manchester United
Speaker 2 Like: Bono and U2, Alicia Keys, Christina Aguilera
Speaker 3 Like: Pelé
Speaker 4 Like: Salma Hayek
 Don't like: Tom Cruise

b Divide the class into pairs. Ask a stronger pair to read out the example dialogue. Draw students' attention to the use of the question and short answer forms and also the use of positive and negative adjectives. Monitor and check students are asking and answering correctly, making a note of any repeated errors to go through as a class after the exercise.

Stronger classes: They can use the people from the photos in Exercise 7a or they can think of other famous people they like / don't like.

They all want to go ...

8 ## Read and listen

Warm up

Ask students if they can remember the name of Nick's band from Exercise 1 (4Tune) and elicit the answer. Students can then read, listen and check their predictions.

a 🔊 Students read the question. Elicit suggestions. Play the recording while students read and listen and check their answer.

TAPESCRIPT
See the photo story on page 24 of the Student's Book.

Answer
Amy, Alex, Chris and Mark want to go to the concert.

(b) Students read through sentences 1 to 4. Go through the first item as an example, if necessary.

Stronger classes: They can do this from memory, reading and listening to check only. They can then correct the false statements.

Weaker classes: Play the recording again while students read and listen. Give students time to complete the exercise. Play the recording again, pausing after each answer for students to check.

Answers
1 True
2 False. She thinks they're really great.
3 True
4 False. Alex is on the phone.

┌─ OPTIONAL ACTIVITY ──────────────
In small groups, students can act out the dialogue from the photo story.

9 Everyday English

(a) Students read through expressions 1 to 4. Go through the first item as an example, if necessary.

Stronger classes: They can decide who says them without referring back to the photo story.

Weaker classes: Refer them back to the photo story to find each expression and who said it.

Answers
1 Amy   2 Amy   3 Amy   4 Amy

(b) Discuss the expressions in Exercise 9a as a class and ask students to try and work out how they would say these things in their own language. Are there any similarities with English?

(c) 🔊 Students read through the jumbled dialogue.

Stronger classes: Students close their books and listen to the dialogue. After listening, they open their books again at page 25 and put the dialogue in the correct order.

Weaker classes: They can do this by listening and reading and then putting the dialogue in the correct order.

Vocabulary notebook
Students should note down the expressions from this section and any translations they may find useful.

TAPESCRIPT/ANSWERS

Guess what? There's a new film on at the cinema.
   With Brad Pitt.
Great! I love Brad Pitt.
All my friends want to go. What about you?
Of course I want to go.
So let's go together.
Fantastic. I'm really excited.

10 Write

Warm up

Ask students if they send emails. If so, how often do they send them? What do they write about and who do they send them to and receive them from?

(a) Ask students what is the name of Anna's favourite U2 CD (*The Unforgettable Fire*). Students read the email. Check answers.

(b) Students can prepare this exercise in class and write the email for homework. Students read through the instructions. Elicit from or remind them of how an email is structured:

Informal openings: Hi!, Hello!
Content: Does not have to be split into paragraphs as in a letter.
Signing off: Does not need a full sentence and can just have a name or an informal signing off expression.

Weaker classes: Give them time to plan a draft of their email using the headings from the Student's Book. They can then swap plans and check them before writing up a final version.

Vocabulary notebook
Students can start a section called *Writing emails*. They should note down the key points about writing emails.

She likes Harry Potter

Unit overview

TOPIC: Family and routines

TEXTS
Reading and listening: a famous writer
Listening: to people talking about their families
Reading: Culture in mind: *British families*
Writing: a paragraph about your family

SPEAKING
Talking about your family and asking about habits

LANGUAGE
Grammar: Present simple: positive and negative; questions and short answers; Possessive *'s*; Possessive adjectives
Vocabulary: Family
Pronunciation: /s/, /z/ and /ɪz/

1 Read and listen

If you set the background information as a homework research task ask students to tell the rest of the class what they found out.

BACKGROUND INFORMATION

J. K. Rowling: Is the author of the famous Harry Potter series. She was born Joanne Kathleen Rowling on July 31st 1965, near Bristol, England. She lived in Portugal until the early 1990s when she moved to Edinburgh with her daughter and began work on a book. The idea for Harry Potter is said to have come to her as she was travelling on a train from Manchester to London in 1990. Her proposal for *Harry Potter and the Philosopher's Stone* was rejected by several publishers initially until Bloomsbury accepted it. By the summer of 2000 the first three Harry Potter books had earned almost $480 million in three years. J. K. Rowling is said to be one of the richest women in Britain. The popularity continues and the fifth instalment was published in June 2003, *Harry Potter and the Order of the Phoenix*. The first two books have been made into films and are still breaking box office records.

Harry Potter: He is the young wizard hero of the Harry Potter series. He overcomes evil with his close friends Ron and Hermione and together they solve many mysteries of the wizarding world.

Warm up

You could bring in some copies of the Harry Potter books in English and in the students' own language. It may be interesting for students to compare the covers of the books since the illustrations are very different for each market.

Alternatively, you can ask students if they have read any of the Harry Potter books or seen any of the films. If so, ask them what they thought of them. This can be discussed in L1.

a Students read the question. Elicit suggestions but do not give the answers at this point. Students read the magazine article to check their answer.

TAPESCRIPT
See text on page 26 of the Student's Book.

Answer
She is the famous writer, J. K. Rowling.

b 🔊 Students read through statements 1 to 6. Go through the first item as an example, if necessary. Play the recording while students listen and read the article again. Students then complete the exercise. Check answers.

Stronger classes: They can do this from memory and can then correct the false statements.

Weaker classes: They can listen and read the text again before completing the exercise. Play the recording again, pausing after each answer to allow students time to check their answers.

Answers
1 False. She's British.
2 False. She lives with her husband, son and daughter.
3 True
4 False. She has a computer but she always writes with a pen first.
5 False. He doesn't like them or their son Dudley.
6 False. He is very happy there.

c In small groups, students discuss their opinions of Harry Potter. If they did the *Warm up*, remind them of the things they said then and see if they can expand their opinions. Ask groups to feedback to the class.

OPTIONAL ACTIVITY

Stronger classes: In pairs, students can think of famous authors and books/plays they have written. They then give their partner either the name of the person or book/play and their partner has to guess the other piece of information.

Weaker classes: Students can match the following famous authors to the following books:

William Shakespeare: *Othello, Hamlet, Macbeth* etc.
Miguel de Cervantes: *Don Quijote*
Leo Tolstoy: *War and Peace*
George Orwell: *Animal Farm*
Aldous Huxley: *Brave New World*
Jane Austen: *Pride and Prejudice*

2 Grammar

Present simple: positive and negative

(a) **Stronger classes:** Students read through sentences 1 to 4. Point out that the verbs have been underlined in items 1 and 2 and students must underline the verbs in items 3 and 4. Ask students to identify the positive and negative verb forms in the sentences and to explain the difference between the two forms (the negative form uses the auxiliary *don't/doesn't*). Ask them too what they notice about the verb form in item 3 (it is third person singular and has an *–s* on the end).

Weaker classes: Books closed. Write two present simple positive and two negative sentences of your own on the board (e.g. *I like English. / They don't like English. / He speaks English. / She doesn't speak French.*). Ask for volunteers to come out and underline the verb in each sentence. Then ask them what they notice about the verbs in each sentence and elicit the difference between positive and negative and singular and plural forms. Students then open their books at page 27 and read through the example sentences and underline the verbs in items 3 and 4.

(b) Students read through the gapped table. Give them a few minutes to complete it. Remind them to think carefully about the verb endings they will need. Check answers.

Answers
Positive: read
Negative: don't read, doesn't read

(c) Students read through the table and complete the missing spellings. Check answers.

Answers
+s: stops, lives, plays
+es: finishes, goes

> **Language note**
> Remind students that in the present simple form the third person singular is the only form which changes and we add one of the endings from the box in Exercise 2c to form it.

(d) This exercise can be set for homework. Students read through sentences 1 to 6. Check any problems. Go through the example as a class. Students complete the exercise. Remind them to look carefully at the subject of the sentence before they choose the verb form they need. Check answers.

Answers
2 don't like
3 studies
4 doesn't speak
5 doesn't listen
6 don't study

Present simple: questions and short answers

(e) Students read through the four questions. Ask them what they notice about the present simple question form in English and elicit that the auxiliary *do* or *does* is used.

(f) Students read through the gapped table. Give them a few minutes to complete it. Check answers.

Answers
Question: Do
Short answer positive: does, do
Short answer negative: don't

(g) This exercise can be set for homework. Students read through items 1 to 5. Check any problems. Go through the example as a class, if necessary. Students complete the exercise. Check answers.

Answers
2 Does   3 Do   4 Do   5 Does

Grammar notebook
Remind students to start a section called *Present simple* in their notebooks and to note down some example sentences and the rules from the section.

3 Pronunciation

/s/, /z/ and /ɪz/

(a) 🔊 Students read through the verbs in the box. Go through the examples as a class, making sure students can hear the difference between each ending. Drill each sound, if necessary.

Stronger classes: They can try to classify each verb and then listen and check only.

Weaker classes: Play the recording once and then play it a second time for students to complete the exercise.

Check answers, playing and pausing the recording after each verb.

TAPESCRIPT/ANSWERS
/s/: stops, works, likes
/z/: goes, reads, learns, gives
/ɪz/: watches, studies, finishes

(b) 🔊 Play the recording again, pausing after each verb for students to repeat.

4 Speak

a Divide the class into pairs. Ask a stronger pair to demonstrate the example dialogue. Remind students of the different short answer forms or elicit them. Students complete the exercise. Monitor and check students are asking and answering correctly, making a note of any repeated errors to go through as a class after the exercise.

b Students read through items 1 to 5. Check any problems. Students complete the exercise. Check answers.

Answers
2 c   3 b   4 a   5 d

c Divide the class into pairs or students can work in the same pair as they did in Exercise 4a. Go through the example as a class, pointing out the use of the third person singular verb forms. Students ask their partner their questions and then note their answers. Monitor and check students are taking turns to ask and answer and gather the information. Then ask pairs to report back to the rest of the class on what they found out about their partner. If students are still having problems with the third person singular forms then revise this area after the exercise.

5 Vocabulary

Family

Warm up

This can be done in L1 if necessary. Ask students how many people are in their family and if they have brothers and sisters. If so, how many? Do they have grandparents?

a Books closed. Elicit any words students know for members of the family in English and write them on the board. Students then open their books at page 28 and look at the words in the box in Exercise 5a. If students have not produced those words already then ask a stronger student to explain what they are. Students then read through the gapped text. Go through the first item as an example. Students complete the exercise. Remind them they can refer back to the reading text on page 26 if necessary. Check answers.

Answers
mother/father, father/mother, aunt/uncle, uncle/aunt

b (🔊) Students read through the words in the box. Check any problems. Go through the example as a class. Students complete the exercise. Check answers.

TAPESCRIPT
Sally: My family's not very big, but it's not small, either! My grandfather's called Fred (we call him Grandad), and my grandmother's called Susan, but we call her Gran. Then there's my mother, Mary, and

my father, Alan. Of course, we call them Mum and Dad! My dad has a brother, he's called uncle Mike, and he's married to Diane, so she's our aunt and they've got a son ... who's our cousin, Tony. Er ... I've got a brother, James, and a big sister, Kate, so I'm in the middle! They're nice, but sometimes James is a pain.

Answers
Grandfather – Fred
Grandmother – Susan
Mother – Mary
Father – Alan
Uncle – Mike
Aunt – Diane
Brother – James
Sister – Kate
Cousin – Tony

Vocabulary notebook
Remind students to start a section called *Family* and to note down the new words from this section.

┌─ **OPTIONAL ACTIVITY** ─────────────
Pairs or small groups. Students must describe a family member without using the relationship word. For example:

S1: I am my mother's brother.
S2: Uncle.

The student who guesses correctly takes the next turn. Monitor and check students are taking turns to ask and answer.

Weaker classes: Students can write down their definitions before they start the activity.

6 Grammar

Possessive *'s*

a **Stronger classes:** Students read the examples. Ask them to explain why the possessive *'s* is used in both cases (it is the name belonging to my father / they are the parents belonging to my father). Ask students to give a few examples of their own using the possessive *'s* and some of their classmates' personal belongings.

Weaker classes: Books closed. Write the words: *Sally's family* on the board. Elicit or explain why the possessive *'s* is used in this example (because it is referring to the family belonging to Sally). Students now open their books at page 28 and look at the examples on the page. Follow the procedure for Stronger classes from this point.

b Students look at the pictures. Check any problems. Students complete the exercise. They can then compare answers in pairs before a whole class check.

Answers
2 Jane's house
3 Mr Wood's car
4 My father's computer
5 My sister's bike
6 My brother's school

Language notes

1. Students may find it useful to note down the following rules of the possessive 's. It is used with:
   - person + thing: *John's book*
   - person + person: *my mum's brother*

   It is not used with:
   - thing + thing: NOT ~~The TV programme's start.~~ We say: *The start of the TV programme.*

2. Students may produce statements like the ~~sister of Sally~~ so it may be useful for them to think about how they express the possessive in their language to make them more aware of the differences in English.

OPTIONAL ACTIVITY

Go round the class picking up various (small) items belonging to students. Hold them up and ask *Whose is it?* Ask a student to reply using the possessive 's. For example:

T: Whose is it? (holding up bag)
S1: It's Maria's.

You can either give the next object to the student who asks the question and chooses who is to reply or you can continue asking the question yourself.

Possessive adjectives

c **Stronger classes:** Students read through the examples. Ask them to underline the possessive adjective in each example and ask students to explain why each one is used (because it refers back to the subject and depending on whether the subject is male or female, singular or plural *his*, *her* or *their* is used).

Weaker classes: Books closed. Write the following example on the board (or one of your own): *I like your bike. He likes her pen.* Ask a student to come out and underline the possessive adjective in each example and then elicit or explain why each one is used. Students open their books at page 29 and read through the example sentences. Follow the procedure for Stronger classes from this point.

d Students read through the gapped table. Go through the examples as a class, pointing out the subject pronouns and the possessive adjectives. Students complete the exercise.

Weaker classes: It may be useful to write the subject pronouns on the board and the possessive adjectives in a jumbled order. Ask students to come out and write the relevant possessive adjective beside the subject pronoun.

Check answers.

Answers
Singular: my, your, his, its
Plural: your, their

e This exercise can be set for homework. Students read through items 1 to 6. Go through the example as a class, asking students to explain why the answer is *My*. Students complete the exercise. Check answers, asking students to justify their choice of possessive adjective.

Answers
1 your   2 His   3 Their   4 her   5 our   6 your

Grammar notebook
Remind students to start a section for *Possessive 's* and *Possessive adjectives* and to note down the examples from this section or some of their own.

OPTIONAL ACTIVITY

You can do a similar activity here as the possessive 's Optional activity. Collect up some small belongings from students. This time students must point to the person it belongs to and answer using the possessive adjective. For example:

T: Whose is it?
S1: It's her bag. etc.

7 Speak

a Divide the class into pairs. Ask a stronger pair to demonstrate the example dialogue. Remind students to refer back to Sally's family tree in Exercise 5 to help them with their questions. Students ask and answer questions. Monitor and check students are taking turns to ask and answer and that they are using the correct possessive adjectives and the possessive 's. Make a note of any repeated errors to go through as a class after the exercise.

b Students draw their family tree, using Sally's one as a model. Remind them not to write in the names of the members of their family, only father, mother etc.

c Divide the class into pairs or students can work in the same pairs they did in Exercise 7a.

Ask a stronger pair to read out the example using their own family trees. Remind students that they must ask the question and then fill in the information in the correct place in their partner's family tree. Students complete the exercise.

Ask pairs to feedback to the class about their partner's family.

OPTIONAL ACTIVITY

Students can decorate their family trees for homework or add photos of the members of the family. These can then be displayed on the classroom wall. Students could vote for the best family tree.

8 Listen

a Students read through items a to f and look at the pictures. Check any problems. Go through the first item as an example if necessary. Students complete the exercise. Check answers.

Answers

1 b 2 a 3 d 4 e 5 c 6 f

(b) 🔊 Explain that students will hear Mark talking about Sally's family and using the expressions in Exercise 8a. Students must put the expressions in Exercise 8a in the order he mentions them. Play the recording while students listen. Play the recording again, pausing as necessary for students to note down the correct order. Check answers, playing and pausing the recording again as necessary.

TAPESCRIPT

Sally I really like my family – they're great! Well, not James, of course.

Mark James? Why? Is he a problem?

Sally Yes, sometimes. You know, I don't _hate_ him, but you know, he doesn't like the TV programmes that I like, things like that. We just … want to do different things. We have a lot of fights!

Mark Right! Sounds normal! And your sister – do you like her?

Sally Kate? Yeah, she's wonderful. I really, really like her. We do lots of things together. We go to the cinema together, erm … we go for walks together …

Mark That's great. That's like me and my brother.

Sally Uh huh. And me and my mum too, we get on really well. We go shopping together, on Saturdays, usually.

Mark What about your dad?

Sally My dad? He's OK. He works in a factory in town. He really doesn't like it!

Mark Does your mum work too?

Sally Yeah, she does. She works in a shop. She sells newspapers …

Answers

5, 6, 2, 1, 4, 3

Culture in mind

If you set the background information as a homework research task ask students to tell the rest of the class what they found out.

BACKGROUND INFORMATION

Canterbury: Is a city in the region of Kent in south east England. It is famous for its university and its cathedral. Chaucer's _Canterbury Tales_ are set there.

Manchester: Is a large city in the north west of England. It is famous for many things including textiles and its two football teams: Manchester United and Manchester City. It hosted the Commonwealth Games in 2002.

Pakistan: Is officially called the Islamic Republic of Pakistan and is in Asia. It is bordered by India to the east, the Arabian Sea to the south, Iran to the south west, Afghanistan to the west and north and Jammu and Kashmir to the north east. The capital is Islamabad and other important cities include Karachi, Lahore and Rawalpindi. Islam is the dominant religion and Urdu is the official language although English is used in many parts of the country. There are many Pakistani communities all over Great Britain.

9 Read

Warm up

Ask students how many people are in their family and how many people live at home with them (e.g. grandparents and parents or only parents?). Ask students to discuss the types of houses/flats they live in. This can be discussed in L1 if necessary.

(a) Pre-teach any vocabulary necessary before students read the texts, e.g. _dishwasher_, _part time_, _parents-in-law_.

Stronger classes: Students read the text quickly. Check any problems. Give students a few minutes to match the texts to the pictures.

Weaker classes: The texts can be read aloud as a class and the matching can be done in pairs.

Check answers.

Answers

The Ashraf family is from Manchester and the Carter family is from Canterbury.

(b) **Stronger classes:** Students can read the text again if necessary and complete the information in the table.

Weaker classes: Divide the class into pairs. Go through the table headings and look at the example. Students complete the exercise.

Check answers.

Answers

Ashraf family: City: Manchester, Number of children: four, Father's job: works in a shop
Carter family: City: Canterbury, Number of children: two, Mother's job: works part time at a hospital, Father's job: works with computers

(c) In small groups, students discuss this question. Ask groups to feedback to the rest of the class.

10 Write

Warm up

Ask students if they have a web page or know anyone who has. Ask them to predict the kind of information they might find on a web page.

a **Stronger classes:** Students look at the pictures and read the text then write the names under the appropriate picture.

Weaker classes: The text can be read aloud as a class. Elicit the first name as an example. Students complete the exercise. Check answers.

Answers
1 Jenny
2 Arthur and Lynne
3 Mark
4 Andy
5 Susan
6 Annie

b **Stronger classes:** Students plan and write a web page based on the model in the Student's Book. Remind them to look carefully at the structure of the text and to identify the topic of each paragraph before they begin.

Weaker classes: Go through each paragraph with the students, eliciting the main topic for each. Put the topic headings on the board. Students then plan and draft their information. Students can write their final versions for homework.

Module 1 Check your progress

1 Grammar

(a) 2 My friends are great singers.
3 London is a fantastic city.
4 Polish restaurants are really good.

(b) 2 doesn't 3 Are 4 isn't 5 Does 6 Is
7 aren't 8 don't

(c) 2 our 3 my, your 4 Her 5 their

(d) 2 How 3 Who 4 Why 5 Where

(e) 2 speaks 3 watch 4 finishes 5 goes 6 listen

2 Vocabulary

(a) 2 Belgium 3 Britain 4 Italy 5 Poland
6 Turkey 7 Japan 8 Canada

(b) 2 Belgian 3 British 4 Italian 5 Polish
6 Turkish 7 Japanese 8 Canadian

(c) 2 singers 3 people 4 women 5 teachers

(d) 2 e 3 b 4 a 5 d 6 c

(e) In the classroom: pen, cassette, notebook, book, chair, pencil, door

Family: parents, aunt, father, daughter, cousin, uncle, mother

Numbers: twenty-one, fourteen, thirteen, seventy, eight, two, thirty

3 Everyday English

2 Let's go together
3 that's right
4 I don't understand
5 Guess what

How did you do?
Check that students are marking their scores. Collect these in and check them as necessary and discuss any further work needed with specific students.

Module 2
People and places

See Introduction.

YOU WILL LEARN ABOUT ...

Ask students to look at the photos on the page and to read through the topics in the box. Check any problems. In small groups, students discuss which topic area they think each photo matches.

Answers
1   Chimpanzees and humans
2   Famous English cities
3   Food around the world
4   British teenagers and TV
5   Two different teenagers

YOU WILL LEARN HOW TO ...

See Introduction.

Use grammar

Go through the example as a class.

Stronger classes: They should be able to continue with the other items on their own or in pairs.

Weaker classes: Put the grammar headings on the board and give an example of your own for each item, e.g. *Stand up! My desk is opposite the board. I've got one brother. Three apples and some pasta. This is your book. I'd like some chicken, please. I go to school every day.*

In pairs, students now match the grammar items in their book. Check answers.

Answers
Imperatives: Buy a travel card and take the tube.
Prepositions of place: The station is opposite the park.
have / has got: I've got three sisters.
Countable/Uncountable nouns: An apple and some sugar.
this, that, these, those: These are your chips.
I'd like / Would you like ...?: I'd like some apples, please.
Present simple / adverbs of frequency: Judy never goes to school.

Use vocabulary

Write the headings on the board. Go through the items in the Student's Book and check understanding. Ask students if they can think of one more item for the *Places in towns* heading. Elicit some responses and add them to the list on the board. Students now do the same for the other headings. Some possibilities are:

Places in towns: *bank, supermarket, library, swimming pool, school*

Parts of the body: *arm, foot, knee, neck, hand*

Food: *chicken, beef, pasta, rice, oranges, bananas*

Days of the week: *Tuesday, Wednesday, Thursday, Friday, Sunday*

TV programmes: *cartoons, soap operas, football / sports programmes*

5 Where's the café?

1 Read and listen

If you set the background information as a homework research task ask students to tell the rest of the class what they found out.

BACKGROUND INFORMATION

London: Is the capital city of England and Great Britain. It is in the south east of England and is made up of 32 boroughs. The city offers many attractions, including the British Museum, the National Gallery, the Tate Gallery and the Victoria and Albert Museums. Other tourist attractions include Buckingham Palace, the Houses of Parliament and Westminster Abbey.

The River Thames: Is one of the main rivers in England. It flows from the Cotswold Hills in the west of England through Oxford, Reading and central London to the North Sea. There are more than twelve bridges spanning the Thames.

The London Eye: Is the world's highest observation wheel. A 30-minute flight in one of its steel and glass capsules offers amazing views over London and on a clear day people can see over seven counties.

The Tube / London Underground: The Metropolitan Railway was opened on January 10th 1863. London has one of the most extensive underground railway systems with 272 stations, nine lines and a route length of 404 kms. 159 kms are underground. The

London underground is expanding and existing lines are being extended and new stations added.

Camden: Is one of London's boroughs on the north side of the river. The railway stations King's Cross, Saint Pancras and Euston are in this borough as well as the British Museum. It is also home to Hampstead Heath and a part of Regent's Park.

Natural History Museum: Is one of London's tourist attractions, popular with families. It is the UK's leading museum of nature.

Warm up

Ask students if they have ever been to London. If so, ask them to tell the class what they saw and where they went. If not, ask them to name some of the major attractions in London.

🔊 Pre-teach any vocabulary, e.g. *tour*, *flight*, *sights*, *travel card*, *tube*, *fashionable*, *collection*, *concert*.

Stronger classes: Students can read the sentences quickly and match them to the pictures.

Weaker classes: Give students a few minutes to read the texts or read them aloud as a class. Do the first item as an example. Students complete the exercise.

Play the recording for students to listen and check their answers.

TAPESCRIPT
See reading text on page 36 of the Student's Book.

Answers
2 d   3 a   4 e   5 c   6 f

2 Vocabulary

Numbers 100 +

🔊 Books closed. Elicit as many numbers as students know in English above 100 and write the numbers and words on the board. Students now open their books at page 37 and look at the numbers. Play the recording, pausing after each number for students to repeat.

TAPESCRIPT
a hundred and twenty
a hundred and fifty
two hundred
three hundred
five hundred
a thousand
two thousand

── OPTIONAL ACTIVITY ──────

Stronger classes: In pairs, students can give each other some sums using numbers above 100. Monitor and check students are taking turns to ask and answer and that they are giving the right answers!

Weaker classes: Divide the class into pairs. You can give pairs sums and the first pair to get the most sums correct in a time limit is the winner.

Vocabulary notebook
Remind students to make a note of these new numbers under their *Numbers* section.

3 Pronunciation
/ð/ and /θ/

🔊 Play the recording while students listen. Ask them if they notice the difference between the two sounds. If students are having problems with the difference then remind them to position their tongue behind their front teeth for the /ð/ sound and to put their tongue between their front teeth, slightly sticking out for the /θ/ sound.

Play the recording again if necessary to give students more practice.

TAPESCRIPT
/ð/ there   mother   the   father
/θ/ thousand   thirty   think   three

4 Grammar
there's / there are

(a) **Stronger classes:** Students read through the examples. Ask them to identify the positive forms and the question forms.

Ask them what they notice about the verbs in each sentence and elicit that *are* is used with plural nouns and *is* with singular nouns. At this point, ask students if they can work out how to form the negative and elicit the rule from them. Students then complete the table and the rule.

Weaker classes: Books closed. Write some examples of your own on the board, e.g. *There are thirty students in this class. There's a bird in the garden. Is there a book on your desk? Are there any students outside?*

Ask students to identify the different forms and elicit or explain when each is used. Students open their books at page 37 and look at the examples. Go through the table as a class, asking students for the

correct words to complete it. Students can then complete the rule.
Check answers.

Answers
Singular nouns: is
Plural nouns: are (some)
Are
are
aren't
Rule: is, are, questions

(b) Students read through sentences 1 to 7. Go through the examples as a class. Students complete the exercise. Remind them to check carefully on the form they need before they fill in the verb. Check answers.

Answers
3 There are   4 There isn't   5 There's   6 There aren't any   7 There aren't any

5 Vocabulary
Places in towns
Warm up

Books closed. Elicit as many names of places in towns as students know in English. Are there any similarities with their own language?

(a) 🔊 Students open their books at page 38 and look at the pictures and the list of words in the box. Go through the example as a class. Students complete the exercise. Play the recording, for students to listen and check their answers. Play the recording a second time if necessary, pausing for students to repeat.

TAPESCRIPT/ANSWERS
1 library   2 railway station   3 supermarket
4 chemist   5 bank   6 bookshop   7 park
8 post office   9 newsagent

(b) Divide the class into pairs. Ask a stronger pair to demonstrate the example dialogue. Draw students' attention to the question and answer forms with *there is/are*. Students ask and answer questions about their town. Monitor and check students are taking turns and that they are using the correct question and answer forms. Make a note of any repeated errors to go through as a class after the exercise.

(c) Divide the class into pairs. Students read through the items in the box. Check any problems. Do the first item as an example, encouraging students to refer back to the places in Exercise 5a. Students complete the exercise. Check answers.

Answers
You send a parcel in a post office.
You catch a train at a railway station.
You buy stamps at a post office.

You change money in a bank.
You buy milk in a supermarket.
You play football in a park.
You buy a magazine in a newsagent.

Language notes
You can explain to students that sometimes in English we refer to *the chemist's* or *the newsagent's* and the word has an apostrophe *s* at the end. This refers to the *chemist's shop* or the *newsagent's shop*.

Students may find it useful to look at the words for *Places in towns* and see if any are similar in their own language.

Vocabulary notebook
Encourage students to start a section called *Places in towns* to note down the new words from this section. Students could also write translations or illustrate each word.

6 Grammar
Positive imperatives

a **Stronger classes:** Students read through the examples. Before they look at the rule box, see if they can work out the rule.

Weaker classes: Books closed. Give students a few simple instructions in English, e.g. *Stand up!, Sit down!, Touch your nose.* etc. Ask students what they noticed about the verb you used in each instruction and elicit that it is the base form without *to*. Students now open their books at page 38 and read through the examples and the rule.

Language note
Students may find it useful to compare how positive imperatives work in their own language. Remind them that we always use the infinitive without *to* for all persons in English, the positive imperative does not change.

b Students read through items 1 to 6 and a to f. Check any problems. Go through the example as a class, if necessary. Students complete the exercise. Check answers.

Answers
2 b   3 e   4 a   5 c   6 d

c Explain to students that you are going to give them some simple instructions using positive imperatives. However, you are going to say [Your name] says Stand up! And students must perform the action. If you give the instructions without saying [your name] before the instruction students should not do the instruction. If a student follows the instruction and you have not given your own name before it, they must sit out of the rest of the game.

Grammar notebook
Remind students to note down the rules for positive imperatives and some examples from this section in their notebooks.

7 Listen, read and speak
Directions

Look box
Go through the prepositions in the box with students before they start Exercise 7a. Explain the difference between *next to* and *near* (in the dialogue) in L1 if necessary.

a 🔊 Students look at the map and quickly read through the dialogue. Check any problems. Play the recording while students listen and read. Give them a few minutes to mark the places on the map before checking answers.

Weaker classes: If necessary, play the recording a second time, pausing after each place is mentioned to give them time to write the names on the map. Check answers.

Play and pause the recording again as necessary to clarify any problems.

TAPESCRIPT
See dialogues on page 39 of the Student's Book.

Answers
1 bank   2 post office   3 railway station

b Divide the class into pairs. Go through the example as a class. Explain to students that they must decide in their pairs where each place is on the map in relation to other places. Monitor and check students are taking turns to say where things are and that they are using the places and prepositions correctly. Note down any repeated errors, to go through as a class after the exercise.

Ask pairs to feedback to the class.

Vocabulary notebook
Students should start a section called *Prepositions of place* and note down the new words from this section. Encourage them to write translations or to illustrate each preposition.

OPTIONAL ACTIVITY
Divide the class into pairs. Students take turns to choose a place on the map without telling their partner. They then describe the place to their partner using directions and prepositions of place and their partner must guess where they are. Monitor and check students are taking turns to ask and answer and that they are using the correct directions and prepositions.

I have no idea!

8 Read and listen

Warm up

Ask students if anyone in their town/city has ever asked them for directions. This can be done in L1.

(a) 🔊 Students read the questions. Check any problems. They then read the text quickly and find the answers.

Play the recording while students read and listen to check their answers. Play the recording again, pausing after each answer, if necessary.

TAPESCRIPT
See the photo story on page 40 of the Student's Book.

Answers
Alex does something stupid. He gives someone directions but doesn't know if they are right or not.

(b) Students read through questions 1 to 4. Check any problems.

Stronger classes: They can do this from memory and then they can read and listen to check their answers.

Weaker classes: Go through the first question as a class. Play the recording for students to read and listen. Students then answer the questions. Check answers, playing and pausing the recording again as necessary.

Answers
1   He wants to know if there is a chemist nearby.
2   No, he doesn't.
3   She thinks it was a stupid thing to do.
4   Alex realises the man is his new Biology teacher.

┌─ OPTIONAL ACTIVITY ──────────────
In small groups, students can act out the dialogue from the photo story.

9 Everyday English

(a) Ask students to find the expressions in the photo story and to decide who says them.

Weaker classes: Go through the first expression as a class, locating it in the photo story.

Students can then translate the expressions into their own language. Remind students to look carefully at the context of each one in the photo story before deciding how it is said in their own language. Check answers as a class.

Answers
1 Alex   2 Amy   3 Amy   4 Alex

(b) Students read the dialogues. Check any problems. Go through the first dialogue as an example, if necessary. Students complete the exercise. Check answers.

Answers
1   You're welcome
2   Wait a minute
3   I have no idea
4   Are you sure

Vocabulary notebook
Students should note down these expressions in their *Everyday English* section.

┌─ OPTIONAL ACTIVITY ──────────────
Stronger classes: Students can write their own short dialogues using the expressions in Exercise 9. They can then act them out in pairs.

Weaker classes: They can act out the dialogues from Exercise 9 in pairs.

10 Write

The writing task can be set for homework or the preparation can be done in class and Exercise 10b can be set for homework.

If you set the background information as a homework research task ask students to tell the rest of the class what they found out.

BACKGROUND INFORMATION

Cambridge: Is a city in the east of England situated on the river Cam. It is an ancient market town with a lot of high-tech and computer businesses on its outskirts. It is also the site for Cambridge University, founded in the twelfth century.

The Fitzwilliam Museum: Is the art museum of the University of Cambridge. It was founded in 1816 and it houses magnificent collections of art and antiquities of national and international importance.

(a) Students read the text silently and match the paragraphs with the headings. Check answers.

Answers
1 B   2 A   3 C

(b) **Stronger classes:** Give students time to plan and draft notes about their own town or city. Remind them to use Rob's text as a model.

Weaker classes: They can discuss their drafts in pairs and then write a rough version of their text. They can swap texts with a partner to check before writing the final version.

┌─ OPTIONAL ACTIVITY ──────────────
Students can add a photo or an illustration of their town or city to their writing and the class could vote for the best one.

6 They've got brown eyes

Unit overview

TOPIC: Describing people

TEXTS
Reading and listening: an article about people and chimpanzees
Listening: to descriptions of people; to personal information
Reading: Culture in mind: *Pets in the UK*
Writing: descriptions of family members

SPEAKING
Asking and answering about things you've got
Describing people
Giving personal information

LANGUAGE
Grammar: *has/have got*; *why ...? because ...*
Pronunciation: /v/
Vocabulary: Colours; Parts of the body

1 Read and listen

a Pre-teach any vocabulary necessary, e.g. *intelligent, fingers, thumb, chocolate, chimpanzee, forests, DNA*.

Students read the questions and look at the pictures. Ask them to predict their answers. Students then read the text and check their answers. Were their predictions correct?

Answers
Chimpanzee: Sally
Girl: Paula

b 🔊 Students read through statements 1 to 4. Check any problems.

Stronger classes: They can do this from memory and can listen and check only. They can then correct the false statements.

Weaker classes: Play the recording while students read and listen. Students complete the exercise. Play the recording again, pausing after each answer for students to check. Students can then correct the false statements.

TAPESCRIPT
See reading text on page 42 of the Student's Book.

Answers
1 False. They haven't got big families.
2 False. She's got two sisters.
3 False. She loves her sisters.
4 False. It's 98% the same.

2 Grammar

why ...? because ...

a **Stronger classes:** Students read the example questions and answer. Point out the use of *why* in the question and *because* in the answer. Elicit or explain that *because* answers the question *why* in English and is followed by a reason. Students then read the second question and re-read the text on page 42 to find the answer. Check answers.

Weaker classes: Books closed. Write the following questions and answer on the board (or an example of your own): *Why are we here? Because we want to learn English.* Draw students' attention to the use of the question word *why* and the answer with *because.* Elicit or explain that *because* answers the question *why* in English and is followed by a reason. Students open their books at page 43. Follow the procedure for Stronger classes.

Check answers as a class.

Answer
Because she loves chocolate.

has/have got

b Go through the examples as a class. Ask students to identify the positive and negative singular forms and the positive plural form. Ask them what they notice about each verb and elicit that the positive singular form is *has got*, the positive plural form is *have got* and negative singular is *hasn't got*. Ask students to work out at this point what they think the plural negative form will be (*haven't got*).

Students now read through the table and complete the gaps. Check answers.

Answers
Negative: haven't got
Question: Has
Short answer: have/haven't, has/hasn't

> **Language notes**
> Explain to students that in short answers with *has/have got* the *got* is dropped and only the *have/has* is used.
>
> Remind students that in British English we usually use *has/have got* with possessions and we say: *I've got a dog.* and NOT ~~I have a dog~~.

c This exercise can be set for homework. Students read through sentences 1 to 6. Go through the first item as an example, if necessary. Students complete the exercise. Ask students to compare with a partner and then students can feedback to their partner.

Answers
Students' own answers.

3 Pronunciation
/v/ *they've*

a 🔊 Students read through words 1 to 9. Play the recording, pausing after each word for students to repeat. Play the recording a second time if necessary.

TAPESCRIPT
1 they've 2 we've 3 you've 4 I've 5 very
6 five 7 verb 8 video 9 volleyball

b 🔊 Students read sentences 1 to 3. Drill the sentences as a class. Play the recording while students listen and check their pronunciation. Play the recording again, pausing after each sentence for students to repeat.

TAPESCRIPT
1 We've got five very big videos.
2 You've got the wrong verb.
3 I've got volleyball practice today.

4 Speak

Divide the class into pairs. Ask a stronger pair to demonstrate the example dialogue. Students ask and answer about their families. Remind them to use the information they completed in Exercise 2c. Monitor and check students are taking turns asking and answering and that they are using the questions and answer forms correctly. Ask pairs to feedback to the class with the information they found out about their partner. If anyone has found out any interesting information, ask them to give the class more details.

5 Vocabulary
Colours
Warm up

Books closed. Elicit as many colours as students know in English and write them on the board. Ask students to compare the words they know with the words for the same colours in their language.

a 🔊 Students open their books at page 44 and look at the colours. Play the recording, pausing after each colour for students to repeat.

TAPESCRIPT
white   black   brown   pink   grey   red   green
purple   beige   yellow   blue   orange

b Go through the example as a class, drawing students' attention to the use of *there's*. Ask students to give you examples of items round the class. Alternatively this can be done in pairs or small groups.

Vocabulary notebook
Encourage students to start a section called *Colours* and to note down the words for colours from this section.

┌─ **OPTIONAL ACTIVITY** ─────────────
Whole class or small groups. Students can think of colours which are used with famous brands, organisations or TV characters, etc. For example: the Red Cross, the Pink Panther, etc.

If this is done in small groups, set a time limit and the group with the most words after the time limit is the winner.

Parts of the body
Warm up

Elicit as many parts of the body as students know in English. Refer students back to the reading text on page 42 to find some of the parts of the body there (*eyes, nose, fingers, thumb*).

c 🔊 Students read through the words in the box. In pairs, students label the diagram. Play the recording for students to listen and check their answers. Play the recording a second time, pausing after each word for students to repeat.

TAPESCRIPT/ANSWERS
1 leg   2 hand   3 foot   4 finger   5 thumb
6 arm   7 hair   8 face   9 ear   10 nose
11 mouth   12 eye

Vocabulary notebook
Students should start a section called *Parts of the body*. Encourage them to note down the words from this section and to translate them into their own language or to illustrate them.

┌─ **OPTIONAL ACTIVITY** ─────────────
Whole class. This activity revises positive imperatives and parts of the body. Give students instructions, e.g. *Touch your head! Put your hands on your knees*. You can speed things up once students have got the hang of the game. If a student carries out the wrong instruction they must sit out of the game.

You can ask students to come out and call out the instructions.

Describing people

d 🔊 Students read through the words in the box. Go through the examples, if necessary. Writing in their notebooks, students complete the lists with the words from the box. Play the recording for students to listen and check their answers. Play the recording a second time, pausing after each word for students to repeat.

Hair colour: blonde brown red grey fair black
Hair style: straight short curly wavy medium-length long
Eye colour: brown blue grey green

(e) Divide the class into pairs. Students look at the pictures. Ask a stronger pair to demonstrate the example dialogue. Draw students' attention to the use of *has got* in each sentence. Students ask and answer in pairs. Monitor and check students are taking turns to ask and answer and that they are using the third person singular form *has got* correctly. Note down any repeated errors to go through as a class at the end of the exercise. Ask pairs to feedback to the rest of the class.

Vocabulary notebook
Encourage students to start a section called *Describing people* and to make a note of all the words from this section. They can write translations or illustrate them.

── OPTIONAL ACTIVITY ──
Divide the class into pairs. Give students a few minutes to look at their partner. Students then stand back to back and describe their partner to the rest of the class. They must describe their hair colour, eye colour, etc. The rest of the class must decide if they are correct.

6 Listen and speak
Describing people

(a) 🔊 Before students listen, ask them to describe each picture using the words from Exercise 5d. Explain that they will only need to tick two of the four pictures. Play the recording while students listen and tick the pictures described. Check answers.

TAPESCRIPT
1
Boy 1 Hi, John! Do you know the new girl in class 4A?

Boy 2 Hi. The girl in 4A? No, I don't know her. Why?

Boy 1 She's really pretty. She's got, er, dark hair …

Boy 2 Uh huh. What – long dark hair?

Boy 1 No, no, it's short. And, erm, blue eyes I think. She's got really big eyes. She's got a great smile, too.

Boy 2 Oh right. So – what's her name?

2
Girl 1 So, what's your new boyfriend like?

Girl 2 Oh, he's wonderful! He's really tall, and he's got fair hair, not very short, sort of medium length.

Girl 1 Long blonde hair!

Girl 2 No! Medium length and fair, not blonde – quite wavy. And he's got lovely big brown eyes. He's really good-looking!

Girl 1 Oooh! So, when can I meet him?

Answers
Pictures 1 and 4

(b) Go through the example as a class, drawing students' attention to the use of *has got* and the adjectives used to describe people. Give students a few minutes to look through their books and to ask and answer about who they are describing. Monitor and check students are using the verbs and adjectives correctly, making a note of any repeated errors to go through as a class after the exercise.

Giving personal information
Warm up

Books closed. Ask students if they have filled in any forms recently. If so, what were they for and what type of information did they have to fill in? If not, then ask them what sort of information they think they would need to give to join a video club.

(c) 🔊 Students read through the form. Check any problems. Play the recording while students listen only. Play the recording a second time while students complete the form. Students can compare answers in pairs before a whole class check. Play the recording again, pausing after each answer if necessary.

TAPESCRIPT
Girl Hello. Can I help you?

Amy Hi. Yes. I want to join the video club, please.

Girl OK. Erm … what's your first name?

Amy Amy.

Girl Sorry?

Amy A-M-Y. Amy.

Girl OK, thank you. And your surname?

Amy It's Harriman.

Girl How do you spell that, please?

Amy H-A-double R-I-M-A-N.

Girl Amy … Harriman. Good. Thanks. And … how old are you?

Amy Fifteen.

Girl Fine. What's your address, please?

Amy 15, Greys Road, Cambridge.

Girl Sorry – can you repeat that please?

Amy 15 … Greys Road … Cambridge.

Girl 15, Greys Road. How do you spell 'Greys', please?

Amy G-R-E-Y-S.

Girl And what's your telephone number, please?

Amy Three two five … double six one.

Girl OK. Thank you.

Amy I've got a mobile phone too.

Girl Good. What's the number please?

Amy Oh seven five nine one ... one double two ... five three eight.

Girl OK, that's all, thanks.

Answers
Surname: Harriman
Age: 17
Address: 15 Greys Road
Telephone: 325661
Mobile: 07591122538

(d) This exercise can be set for homework. Students read through items 1 to 6. Check any problems. Go through the example, if necessary. Students complete the exercise. Check answers.

Answers
2 What's your first name
3 How do you spell that, please
4 What's your address
5 Can you repeat that, please
6 What's your telephone number, please

(e) Divide the class into pairs. Students ask and answer questions from Exercise 6d. Monitor and check students are taking turns to ask and answer and that they are using the correct question and answer forms.

┌─ OPTIONAL ACTIVITY ─────────────

Stronger classes
They could change their identities and ask and answer using different information.

Weaker classes
Ask pairs from Exercise 6e to imagine they are completing a form to join a club of their choice. Students can act out their dialogues.

Culture in mind

7 Read

Warm up

Ask students if they have any pets. If so, what kinds of animals do they have? Do they know anyone who has a strange or unusual pet? If so, ask students to give you more information. This can be done in L1.

(a) Students look at the photos. Go through the names of each pet before students start the exercise.

Stronger classes: They can read the article silently and answer the question. Go through the first item as an example, if necessary.

Weaker classes: Read the article aloud as a class. Go through the first item as an example then in pairs students can complete the exercise.

Answers
1 M   2 M   3 W   4 W

(b) Students read through questions 1 to 6. Check any problems.

Stronger classes: They can answer these questions without reading the text again and can read and check only.

Weaker classes: Go through the first item as an example. In pairs, students read the text again and complete the exercise.

Check answers as a class.

Answers
1 Almost 50%
2 650,000
3 Snakes, spiders and lizards
4 About £30 million
5 Electrical equipment: stereos, TVs and DVD players
6 Becks, Britney, Batman, Homer, Hobbit, Bilbo Baggins

(c) In pairs or small groups students discuss the question. Ask for feedback. Are there any interesting answers? If so, encourage students to give more information to the rest of the class.

┌─ OPTIONAL ACTIVITY ─────────────

Individual or pairs. Students choose their ideal pet and write about what it is, how they would look after it, what they would call it, what it eats, etc. They can then read out their descriptions to the rest of the class without saying what the animal is. The other students can guess what the animal is.

8 Write

(a) Students read through the two descriptions and match them with the pictures. Check any problems.

Answers
a 1   b 2

(b) This can be set for homework. Encourage students to read Anna's texts again, noting down all the things she mentions about the people she is describing (name, age, eye colour, hair colour and style, things he/she likes, one extra piece of information).

Stronger classes: They can use Anna's models to write their own descriptions.

Weaker classes: Encourage them to write a draft version and to swap with a partner to check. They can then write up their final versions.

┌─ OPTIONAL ACTIVITY ─────────────

Students can add photos or illustrations to their descriptions and these can be displayed around the class.

(7) This is delicious!

Unit overview

TOPIC: Unusual food

TEXTS
Reading and listening: a text about unusual food from around the world
Listening and speaking: ordering food in a restaurant
Reading and listening: photo story: *I'm really hungry!*
Writing: an informal letter

SPEAKING
Talking about food
Ordering food in a restaurant

LANGUAGE
Vocabulary: Food; Everyday English: *I'm really hungry; really?*; *What's wrong?*; *Do you think so?*
Grammar: Countable and uncountable nouns; *this/that/these/those*; *I'd like … / Would you like …?*
Pronunciation: /w/

1 Read and listen

Warm up

Ask students what their favourite food is. Do they have a favourite food from another country? If so, what is it?

Alternatively, you can ask students if they can think of any international words for food that they know. Elicit suggestions and put them on the board.

(a) Students look at the pictures and the countries in the box. Go through each item as a class, making sure students know how to pronounce each word. Go through the first item as an example, if necessary. In pairs, students work out which countries the other items come from. Do not check answers at this stage.

(b) 🔊 Pre-teach any vocabulary, e.g. *restaurant, waiter, disgusting, steak, vinegar, mayonnaise*. Play the recording while students read and listen and check their answers to Exercise 1a. Play the recording again, pausing as necessary after each answer.

TAPESCRIPT
See reading text on page 48 of the Student's Book.

Answers
1e rattlesnake: the USA
2d grasshopper: Mexico
3b chips: Britain
4a alligator: Brazil
5c snails: France
6f kangaroo: Australia

OPTIONAL ACTIVITY
Students can research other countries for homework and find out if there are any other interesting foods people like to eat. They can report their findings to the class the next day.
---

2 Vocabulary

Food

Warm up

Books closed. Ask students if they know the English names for any food items. Elicit suggestions.

(a) 🔊 Students open their books at page 49, look at the picture and read through the words in the box. They can check their predictions from the *Warm up*. Check they understand the different catagories. Play the recording, pausing after each item. Go through the first item from the box as an example, if necessary. Students classify the other items. Check answers.

TAPESCRIPT/ANSWERS
1 chicken
2 apples
3 bananas
4 strawberries
5 tomatoes
6 onions
7 bread
8 eggs
9 cheese

(b) Divide the class into pairs. Ask a stronger pair to demonstrate the example dialogue. Students ask and answer about what they like and don't like. Monitor and check students are taking turns to ask and answer. Ask pairs to feedback to the rest of the class about their partner.

Vocabulary notebook
Students should start a section called *Food* and note down the words from this section. They can either write translations for the items or illustrate each one.

OPTIONAL ACTIVITY
Small groups or whole class. A student begins with a food item. The next student must repeat the first item and add a new item. The game continues in this way until someone can't remember an item in the correct order. For example:

S1: In my bag I have apples.
S2: In my bag I have apples and potatoes.
S3: In my bag I have apples and potatoes and [new item] etc.

Grammar

Countable and uncountable nouns

(a) **Stronger classes:** Students read through the words in the box and look at the table. Ask them what they notice about the words in the Countable column in the table and elicit that they all have *a/an* in front of them. Ask them which word appears before the uncountable nouns (*some*). Ask a student to explain the difference between countable and uncountable nouns if they can. Students now complete the table with the words from the box.

Weaker classes: Books closed. Write the headings countable and uncountable on the board and the nouns *apple* and *cheese*. Ask students if we can count apples and elicit the response, then do the same with cheese. Ask a student to come out and write each noun under the appropriate heading. At this point, elicit which words precede countable nouns (*a/an*) and which words precede uncountable nouns (*some*). Ask students to provide another example for each column at this stage. Students then open their books at page 50 and look through the list of words in the box. Ask volunteers to come out and write the nouns under the relevant heading on the board.

Check answers.

Answers
Countable: tomato, egg, strawberry, orange, chicken, onion
Uncountable: bread, chicken, sugar, beef, rice

OPTIONAL ACTIVITY
To check understanding at this point, call out a few food nouns of your own and ask students to tell you if they are countable or uncountable.

(b) Students can read and complete the rule based on the information they supplied in Exercise 3a.

Answers
an; some

Grammar notebook
Encourage students to note down the rules and some examples of countable/uncountable nouns from this section.

OPTIONAL ACTIVITY
Give students the following items (or others of your own choice) to classify as Countable or Uncountable:
Potatoes (C), apples (C), cheese (U), pasta (U), water (U), orange (C) etc.

---

this/that/these/those

Stronger classes: Students look at the pictures and the sentences. Ask them which words are singular and which are plural and elicit that *this/that* are singular and *these/those* are plural. Then ask a student to explain the difference between them. *This/these* are used when we refer to something closer to the speaker while *that/those* are used when something is further away from the speaker.

Weaker classes: Books closed. Using items in the classroom, give students some examples using *this/that/these/those*. Ask students if they can tell you which are the singular words and which are the plural words. Then elicit or explain when we use *this/these* and *that/those*. Students now open their books at page 50 and look at the pictures and examples there.

(c) Students look at pictures 1 to 4. Go through the first item as an example if necessary. Students complete the exercise. Check answers.

Answers
1 These   2 that   3 Those   4 this

Grammar notebook
Encourage students to note down the rules and some examples from this section. They can write translations for each item if it will help.

I'd like … / Would you like …?

(d) 🔊 Students read through the dialogue quickly. Check any problems. Play the recording while students read and listen to find the answers. Check answers, playing and pausing the recording again as necessary.

TAPESCRIPT
See dialogue on page 51 of the Student's Book.

Answers
He wants to buy apples, strawberries, lettuce, onions and potatoes.

(e) Students read through items 1 to 4. Go through the first item as an example, drawing students' attention to the expressions in the dialogue in Exercise 3d. Students complete the answers. Students can check answers in pairs before a whole class check.

Answers
1 like
2 please, 'd like
3 Would you like
4 thanks

OPTIONAL ACTIVITY
Stronger classes
Students can change the items they want to buy and then act out the dialogue in Exercise 4d in pairs.
Weaker classes
Students can act out the dialogue from Exercise 4d in pairs.

---

4 Pronunciation
/w/ would

🔊 Students read through questions 1 to 4. Check any problems. Play the recording while students listen. Play the recording a second time, pausing after each question for students to repeat.

TAPESCRIPT
1 Would you like a sandwich?
2 Are you the new waiter?
3 What do you want to eat?
4 Where in the world are you from?

5 Listen and speak
Warm up

Ask students if they have ever eaten in a restaurant. If so, when did they eat there? What did they choose from the menu and who were they with?

(a) 🔊 Students read through the menu. Check any problems. Ask students to predict what they think the man and woman on the recording will choose. Play the recording while students listen and tick the items the people order and check their predictions. Check answers, playing and pausing the recording again as necessary.

TAPESCRIPT

Waiter Good afternoon. Are you ready to order now?

Man Yes, I think we are. Darling, what would you like?

Woman I'd like the goat's cheese salad for a starter, please.

Waiter Certainly madam.

Woman Then I'd like the vegetable lasagne, with salad.

Waiter And chips, madam?

Woman No, no chips, thank you. Just lasagne and salad.

Waiter And for you, sir?

Man What is the soup today?

Waiter It's tomato soup, sir. And very good it is too.

Man All right then, I'd like the soup please, and then the chicken.

Waiter Chicken, yes. Chips or potatoes?

Man Chips please, and the vegetables too.

Waiter Certainly. And what would you like to drink?

Man Darling?

Woman Mmm, just tea please.

Man And I'd like an orange juice please.

Waiter Perfect, thank you. So that's soup of the day ...

(b) Students read through the phrases in the box. Check any problems.

Stronger classes: Ask them if they can remember any phrases the waiter or the customer used in the dialogue in Exercise 5a. Remind them to use these when acting out their dialogues.

Weaker classes: Before students begin, play the recording from Exercise 5a again to remind students of the language and structures used.

In groups of three, students take turns to order and take the order in a restaurant. Monitor and check students are taking turns and are asking and answering correctly.

┌─ OPTIONAL ACTIVITY ─────────────

Stronger classes: Students can plan and write their own ideal menus and decorate them. Students can then vote for the best menu.

Weaker classes: Ask groups to act out their dialogues to the rest of the class.

I'm really hungry!

6 Read and listen
Warm up

Ask students how often they eat fast food. If they eat fast food, what kind of fast food do they like?

(a) 🔊 Students read the question. Play the recording while students listen and check their answer (hamburgers).

TAPESCRIPT
See the photo story on page 52 of the Student's Book.

(b) Students read through statements 1 to 5. Check any problems.

Stronger classes: They can complete the exercise and can then listen and check only.

Weaker classes: Go through the example as a class. Play the recording again while students read and listen and then complete the exercise. Play the recording again, pausing after each item for students to check their answers.

Answers
1 d   2 c   3 e   4 a   5 b

7 Everyday English

(a) Students read through expressions 1 to 4.

Stronger classes: They can decide who says which expression and then read and check.

Weaker classes: Play the recording again or read the photo story again. Students then decide who said which expression. Check answers as a class.

Answers

1 Amy   2 Lucy   3 Amy   4 Lucy

(**b**) Students read through dialogues 1 to 4. Check any problems.

Stronger classes: They can complete the exercise.

Weaker classes: Go through the first dialogue as an example, showing students how only one expression from Exercise 7a is possible. Students complete the exercise.

Check answers.

Answers

1 Really
2 I'm really hungry
3 Do you think so
4 What's wrong

Vocabulary notebook

Remind students to note down these expressions and a translation in their *Everyday English* section.

OPTIONAL ACTIVITY ══════════════

Stronger classes: They can write and act out new dialogues using the expressions from Exercise 7a.

Weaker classes: They can act out the dialogues in Exercise 7b.

---

8 Write

(**a**) Explain to students that the letter is from an English family. Ask them where the family lives (London) and what they want to know (what food you like and don't like). Ask them if they know what P.S. means in English (post script, when you add something to the end of a letter that you forgot to include in the main body). Students read the letter and find the answers.

(**b**) This exercise can be set for homework. Encourage students to answer all the questions from the letter on page 53. Students should make notes first and then draft a version of their letter. Remind them of some of the conventions of letter-writing:
- Opening: Dear
- New paragraphs for different topics
- Signing off phrases: Best wishes, Yours sincerely,
- P.S.: This can be added if you forget something in the main body of the letter.

Students complete their letters. They can swap with a partner to check and then write a final version.

Vocabulary notebook

Remind students to note down any new expressions and any points to remember for informal letter writing.

8 I sometimes watch soaps

Unit overview

TOPIC: Television programmes and viewing habits

TEXTS
Reading and listening: a text about different ways of life
Listening: an interview about TV and TV programmes
Reading and listening: Culture in mind: *What British teenagers watch*
Writing: a paragraph about TV

SPEAKING
Talking about regular activities and daily routine
Talking about TV programmes

LANGUAGE
Vocabulary: Days of the week; TV programmes; *What's the time?*
Grammar: Present simple with adverbs of frequency
Pronunciation: Compound nouns

1 Read and listen

If you set the background information as a homework research task, ask students to tell the rest of the class what they found out.

BACKGROUND INFORMATION

Amish: The Amish movement began in the late 17th century and was founded by Jacob Amman. Their way of life is based on attempting to preserve elements of late 17th century rural culture and they reject most developments of modern society. There are approximately 100,000 Amish in 22 US states. Ohio is said to have approximately 45,000. The Amish usually speak a dialect of German called Pennsylvania Dutch but learn English at school. They have no cars, they don't use electricity and have no radios or televisions. Men tend to wear plain dark-coloured suits and women tend to wear plain coloured long-sleeved dresses with bonnets and aprons.

Pennsylvania: Is one of the states of the USA. It is in the mid-Atlantic region and is bordered to the north by Lake Erie and New York, to the east by New Jersey, to the south west by Delaware, Maryland and West Virginia and by Ohio to the west. The capital of Pennsylvania state is Harrisburg and Philadelphia is one of its main cities.

Australia: Is the world's oldest, smallest and flattest continent and the only continent occupied by a single nation. Its capital city is Canberra. It has five states on the mainland (Queensland, New South Wales, Victoria, South Australia and Western Australia) and also Tasmania, an island just off its south coast. The Aborigines (Australian native people) are thought to have come from Australia and Southeast Asia at least 49,000 years ago.

Warm up

Discuss the unit title as a class. Elicit or explain the meaning of soaps (or soap operas) and ask students if they enjoy watching them. Ask them to name some of the more popular soaps in their country.

a Pre-teach any vocabulary students may need to know, e.g. *farm, electricity, buggy*. Students read through the chart. Check any problems. They then look at the pictures and decide which activities they think each person does. This can be done in pairs.

Stronger classes: Students then read the text and check their ideas.

Weaker classes: Read the text aloud as a class to check ideas.

Answers
Joshua
2 ✓ 3 ✓ 4 ✓ 5 ✗
Judy
1 ✓ 2 ✓ 3 ✗ 4 ✗ 5 ✓

b 🔊 Students read through questions 1 to 4. Check any problems.

Stronger classes: They can answer the questions and then listen and read to check answers only.

Weaker classes: Play the recording while students read and listen. Give students a few minutes to complete the exercise. Check answers, playing and pausing the recording again as necessary.

TAPESCRIPT
See the reading text on page 54 of the Student's Book.

Answers
1 Joshua is from Pennsylvania, USA. Judy is from Australia.
2 He never watches TV because they don't have electricity.
3 She never goes to school because she lives 600 kms from the nearest town.
4 In the morning she helps her father and in the evening she watches soaps on TV.

You can give students the following True/False activity on the reading text. Encourage students to correct the false answers.

1 Joshua lives in a school.
2 He always wears simple clothes.
3 He goes to school five days a week.
4 Judy lives 6 kms from the nearest town.
5 She never goes to school and she learns from home.
6 She sometimes talks to her teacher on the TV.

Answers

1 False. He lives on a farm.
2 True
3 True
4 False. She lives 600 kms from the nearest town.
5 True
6 False. She sometimes talks to him on the radio.

2 Vocabulary
Days of the week
Warm up

Books closed. Ask students if they know any of the days of the week in English. If so, write them on the board. Ask students if they notice any similarities between the words in English and their own language.

🔊 Students open their books at page 55 and read through the days of the week in the box. Play the recording, pausing after each day for students to repeat. If students are having problems with any particular day, drill as a class.

TAPESCRIPT

Monday   Tuesday   Wednesday   Thursday
Friday   Saturday   Sunday

> **Language note**
> Listen carefully for students' pronunciation of *Wednesday* and make sure they are pronouncing it /wenzdeɪ/ and not /wednesday/. If there are problems, drill this word a few times in isolation.

Vocabulary notebook

Encourage students to start a section called *Days of the week* and to note down the words in English and a translation if this helps.

Call out a day of the week (e.g. Thursday) and then a student's name. The student must supply you with the next day. That student then calls out another student's name and he/she continues with the next day, etc. For example:

T: Maria, Thursday.
S1: Friday. Pietro.
S2: Saturday. Ana. etc.

3 Grammar
Adverbs of frequency

a Give students a few minutes to read through the words in the box. Elicit or give an example of your own for the first adverb of frequency, then ask students to provide an example of their own for the others. Students then read through items 1 to 7. Check any problems. Go through the example as a class, if necessary. Students complete the exercise. Remind them to refer back to the reading text on page 54 if they need to. Check answers.

Answers

2 never   3 always   4 sometimes   5 often
6 hardly ever   7 always

b **Stronger classes:** Students read through the rule and complete it. Ask them to provide an example of their own or from Exercise 3a for each part of the rule to check they understand.

Weaker classes: They may find it useful to refer back to their completed answers in Exercise 3a to help them complete the rule.

Answers
after; before

> **Language note**
> Students may want to produce statements like ~~Never I go shopping~~. Ask students to compare the position of adverbs of frequency in their own language with English. Remind them that adverbs of frequency always go after the verb *be*, e.g. *I'm always late*, but before any other verbs, e.g. *I never go out at the weekend*.

c Students read through the information in the table and then look at the examples. Ask a few students to give examples of their own using the expressions in the table.

> **Language note**
> Again students may find it useful to compare the position of these expressions with the same expressions in their own language. It may also be useful for students to translate these expressions. Are there any similarities?

d 🔊 Students look at the pictures and sentences 1 to 4. Check any problems. Go through the example as a class, drawing students' attention to the use of the adverbs of frequency expression. Students complete the exercise. Make sure they understand that the sentence they write must mean the same as the first one and must include an adverb of frequency expression. Play the recording while students listen and check their answers.

TAPESCRIPT/ANSWERS

1 My mum checks her email twice a day.
2 Tom eats fish twice a week.
3 Susan goes shopping three times a week.
4 Harry plays football once a week.

4 Speak

Divide the class into pairs. Students read through the items in the box. Check any problems. Ask a stronger pair to demonstrate the example dialogue, drawing students' attention to the use of the adverbs of frequency. Give students a few minutes to ask and answer about the items in the box. Monitor and check students are taking turns to ask and answer and that they are using adverbs of frequency correctly. Make a note of any repeated errors to go through as a class after the exercise. Ask a few pairs to feedback to the class about their partner.

Grammar notebook

Encourage students to start a section called *Adverbs of frequency* and to note down the expressions and rules from this section. They may find it useful to write translations of some of the expressions.

5 Vocabulary

TV programmes

Warm up

Books closed. Ask students how often they watch TV each week. Encourage them to use an expression of frequency from this unit. Are there any interesting results? If so, discuss these as a class.

(a) Students read through the questions. Discuss these as a class and in L1 if appropriate. If there are any particularly interesting answers, discuss these further as a class.

(b) 🔊 Give students a few minutes to look at the pictures and read the programme types. Play the recording, pausing after each word for students to repeat.

Divide the class into pairs. Students now decide on an example for each picture and discuss their favourite type of programme. Ask pairs to feedback to the rest of the class.

TAPESCRIPT

1 soap operas
2 documentaries
3 sports programmes
4 game shows
5 the news
6 chat shows
7 comedies
8 cartoons

┌─ OPTIONAL ACTIVITY ─────────────
Mime game. Students can choose their favourite TV programme and mime the title to the rest of the class or a small group. Students have five guesses to guess the title correctly.

6 Pronunciation

Compound nouns

(a) 🔊 Students read through the words. Play the recording, pausing after each word. Ask students to identify where the stress falls (the first word), making sure they can hear this.

TAPESCRIPT

chat shows
game shows
sports programmes
soap operas

(b) 🔊 Play the recording again, pausing after each word for students to repeat.

7 Listen and speak

(a) 🔊 Students look through the information in the chart. Explain that their answers will consist of expressions of frequency. Play the recording, pausing after the examples to make sure students understand what they have to do. Remind them that each interviewee may not mention every type of programme in the table. Continue with the recording while students listen and complete the chart.

Weaker classes: If necessary, play the recording for Interview 1 and give students time to write their answers then play it a second time for Interview 2, giving students time to complete the table for that part.

Check answers, playing and pausing the recording again as necessary.

TAPESCRIPT

Interview 1

Interviewer   Excuse me. How often do you watch TV?

Person 1   Pardon?

Interviewer   How often do you watch TV?

Person 1   Oh, only sometimes.

Interviewer   For example – twice a week? Three times a week?

Person 1   Erm – I think three times a week, usually. Yes. I hardly ever watch TV at the weekend.

Interviewer   OK. Thanks. And, what do you watch – what kinds of programmes?

Person 1:   Erm – usually sports programmes. And documentaries, sometimes. I like documentaries about animals and nature.

Interviewer   Fine. OK. And – the news?

Person 1   No, I never watch the news. I read a newspaper.

Interviewer   Uh huh. And what about soap operas!

Person 1   No, never! They're terrible!

Interviewer   OK – thank you very much.

Person 1   You're welcome.

Interview 2

Interviewer Excuse me – can we ask you some questions please?

Person 2 Er – what about?

Interviewer Television. We're doing a survey at school.

Person 2 Well, OK – but be quick please!!

Interviewer Oh! OK. Right. Number one – how often do you watch TV?

Person 2 A lot. Every day. Well, maybe not every day – but five or six days a week.

Interviewer Right – that's a lot. And what type of programme do you usually watch?

Person 2 For example?

Interviewer Well – erm – chat shows?

Person 2 No, never.

Interviewer Sports programmes?

Person 2 Hardly ever.

Interviewer Comedies?

Person 2 Sometimes.

Interviewer Cartoons?

Person 2 Oh yeah, great, cartoons. I often watch cartoons.

Interviewer The news?

Person 2 Usually. But please – hurry up!!

Interviewer OK – last one: soap operas?

Person 2 Always.

Interviewer You always watch soap operas?

Person 2 Yes. My favourite is *Coronation Street* – and I'm in a hurry because it starts in 5 minutes! I don't want to miss it. Bye!

Interviewer Oh – OK. Thank you very much. Yes. Bye.

Answers

Interview 1
Documentaries: sometimes
The news: never
Soap operas: never

Interview 2
Chat shows: never
Sports programmes: hardly ever
Comedies: sometimes
The news: usually
Soap operas: always
Cartoons: often

(b) Give students a few minutes to complete the *Me* column with their own information. Ask a few students to feedback to the class.

(c) Divide the class into pairs. Ask a stronger pair to demonstrate the example dialogue, drawing students' attention to the use of the question and answer

forms. Give students time to ask and answer and complete the column for their partner. Monitor and check that students are taking turns to ask and answer and that they are using the correct question forms and frequency expressions in their answers. Note down any repeated errors to go through as a class after the exercise. Ask pairs to feedback to the class on the information they found out about their partner.

┌─ OPTIONAL ACTIVITY ─────────────
In pairs, students can draw up the results of the questions in Exercise 7 as a graph.

8 Vocabulary
What's the time?

Warm up

Ask a stronger student the question *What's the time?* and elicit the response in English if possible. Ask students if they know how to express any other times in English. If so, draw a few clock faces on the board and ask them to come out and write the time in words under them.

(a) 🔊 Students look at the clocks.

Stronger classes: They may be able to write the times under each clock without listening. They can then listen and check only.

Weaker classes: Play the recording, pausing after the example. Play the rest of the recording while students listen and write their answers.

Check answers, playing and pausing the recording again as necessary.

Play the recording again, pausing after each time for students to repeat.

TAPESCRIPT/ANSWERS
1   7.20 (seven twenty)
2   12.00 (twelve o'clock)
3   12.30 (twelve thirty)
4   2.00 (two o'clock)
5   8.45 (eight forty-five)
6   11.15 (eleven fifteen)

┌──────────────────────────────────┐
Language note
Some students may produce times like ~~They are seven and twenty~~. or ~~They are seven twenty~~. because of the way their own language works. Make sure students are clear about how we say times in English.
└──────────────────────────────────┘

(b) 🔊 Draw four clock faces on the board and elicit the o'clock, quarter past, half past and quarter to. Play the recording while students look at the clocks in their books. Then play the recording again, pausing each time for students to repeat.

1 quarter past seven
2 half past seven
3 quarter to eight
4 twenty to six
5 five to seven
6 twenty-five past six

c 🔊 Play the recording while students listen only. Play the recording a second time while students write the time they hear.

Weaker classes: They may find it helpful if the recording is paused after the first speaker and you go through this as an example.

Check answers as a class.

TAPESCRIPT/ANSWERS

1

Girl   Excuse me. What's the time, please?

Boy   The time? Erm ... it's six twenty.

2

Boy   There's a really good film on TV tonight.

Girl   Oh yeah? When?

Boy   Erm ... nine o'clock, I think.

3

Girl   What time's the bus to Cambridge?

Boy   Half past ten.

4

Girl   Do you want to come to the cinema tonight?

Boy   Yeah, OK.

Girl   OK. Come to my house first.

Boy   What time?

Girl   Is quarter past seven OK?

Boy   Yeah, fine. See you then.

Girl   OK. Bye.

Vocabulary notebook

Students should start a section called *Telling the time* and note down the different ways to do this in English.

┌─ **OPTIONAL ACTIVITY** ══════════════

You will need a large world map with time zones for this.

In pairs or small groups. Give students a country and then the time difference in hours. Students then work out what the time will be in that country at the time of your question. The first pair/group to guess choose the next country.

To make this more fun, you can award points for the pair/group who answer first and correctly.

9 # Speak

Students look at the information in the table. Give them a few minutes to complete the *Me* column with their own information. Divide the class into pairs. Students read through the example dialogue. Check any problems. Ask a stronger pair to demonstrate the example question and answer, drawing students' attention to the use of the question *What time do you ...?* Give students a few minutes to ask and answer their questions and then to note down their partner's answers in the *My partner* column of the table. Ask pairs to feedback to the class about their partner.

Culture in mind

10 # Read and listen

If you set the background information as a homework research task, ask students to tell the rest of the class what they found out.

BACKGROUND INFORMATION

Macclesfield: Is a town in north west England, not far from Manchester.

Cheshire: Is a county in the north west of England. It has borders with the Mersey Estuary and Wales. The main town in the county is the city of Chester.

EastEnders: Is a long-running soap opera aired on BBC 1 three evenings a week. The soap is set in the mythical London borough of Walford and features different families who live in 'the square'.

---

a Students look at the pictures and read the questions. Give them a few minutes to read Jane's profile and to complete the table.

Weaker classes: Students can read the text silently or it can be read aloud. Go through the first item in the table in Exercise 10b for Jane as a class. Students complete the exercise, writing their answers in their notebooks. Remind them to refer back to the text on page 58 as necessary.

Check answers.

Answers
Age: 16
Programmes she likes: EastEnders / soap operas, chat shows, films, comedy programmes and documentaries
Programmes she doesn't like: Sports programmes, cartoons, game shows, news programmes
Favourite programme: EastEnders
Number of hours a week she watches TV: 5 or 6 hours a week

b 🔊 Play the recording while students listen and complete the table for Mark, again using their notebooks to write their answers.

Weaker classes: Play the recording once while students listen only. Play it a second time while students complete their answers.

Check answers, playing and pausing the recording again as necessary.

TAPESCRIPT

Interviewer   Hi Mark.

Mark   Hi.

Interviewer   Can you tell us something about yourself?

Mark   Yeah – my name's Mark Fields, and I'm 16.

Interviewer   Do you live in Macclesfield?

Mark   Not really – I live in Congleton, it's near Macclesfield.

Interviewer   Fine. So – tell us about the TV programmes you like. Do you like sports programmes?

Mark   Erm, yeah – I sometimes watch sports programmes. But my favourite programmes are comedies.

Interviewer   Oh right. For example?

Mark   Well, I really like *That 70's Show* – it's my favourite.

Interviewer   Uh huh – that's an American show, isn't it?

Mark   That's right. It's a really good comedy – I love it.

Interviewer   OK. So – what are the programmes that you never watch?

Mark   Never? Erm – well, I hate soap operas, I never watch them, and I don't like documentaries or game shows. They're the ones I never watch.

Interviewer   Fine, thanks. And Mark – how many hours a week do you watch TV?

Mark   Erm, not a lot – about 5 or 6 hours, I think.

Interviewer   Is that on weekdays?

Mark   No, I usually watch TV at the weekends, really.

Interviewer   OK, Mark – thanks.

Mark   No problem.

Answers
Age: 16
Programmes he likes: Sports programmes, comedies, chat shows, films, cartoons, news programmes
Programmes he doesn't like: Soap operas, documentaries, game shows
Number of hours he watches TV: 5 or 6 hours a week

c 🔊 Students read through items 1 to 5. Check any problems. Go through the first item, as an example, playing and pausing the recording after the answer.

Stronger classes: They can underline their answers and listen and check only.

Weaker classes: Play the recording once for students to listen only. Play the recording a second time for students to underline their answers.

Check answers, playing and pausing the recording again as necessary.

Answers
1 Congleton
2 comedy
3 an American
4 5 or 6
5 at the weekends

d In small groups students discuss the questions. Ask groups to feedback to the class.

11 Write

a Ask students what Pavel's favourite programme is, what kind of programme it is and how often he watches it. Give them a few minutes to read Pavel's paragraph. Check answers.

Answers
His favourite programme is a game show called *The Jackpot*. He watches it once a week.

b This exercise can be set for homework. Go through the structure of Pavel's paragraph as a class, eliciting the type of information he has included. Students can draft their paragraph and swap with a partner to check. They can then write a final version.

┌─ OPTIONAL ACTIVITY ──────────────
Stronger classes
They can add more information about their favourite programme and add illustrations or pictures from a magazine.

Module 2 **Check your progress**

1 **Grammar**

(a) 2 There is   3 There are   4 Is there   5 Are there
6 Are there

(b) 2 haven't got   3 have got   4 've got
5 haven't got   6 hasn't got

(c) 2 those   3 these   4 that

(d) 1 some   2 some   3 an   4 a

(e) 2 goes   3 plays   4 eat

(f) 2 a   3 b   4 e   5 c

2 **Vocabulary**

(a) 2 a/one thousand   3 eighty-four   4 thirteen
5 nineteen   6 a/one hundred   7 ninety

(b) Parts of the body: arm, finger, mouth, hand, head
Colours: yellow, red, black, blue, (orange)
Food: butter, chicken, sugar, (orange), beef, eggs

(c) 2 Sunday   3 Monday   4 Wednesday   5 Tuesday
6 Saturday   7 Friday

3 **Everyday English**

2 Are you sure   3 You're welcome   4 I have no
idea   5 Wait a minute   6 What's wrong
7 Do you think so

How did you do?
Check that students are marking their scores. Collect
these in and check them as necessary and discuss any
further work needed with specific students.

Module 3
Free time

See Introduction.

YOU WILL LEARN ABOUT ...

Ask students to look at the photos on the page and to read through the topics in the box. Check any problems. In small groups, students discuss which topic area they think each photo matches.

Answers
1 Sports in British schools
2 A London carnival
3 An athlete in a wheelchair
4 American festivals

YOU WILL LEARN HOW TO ...

See Introduction.

Use grammar

Go through the example as a class.

Stronger classes: Should be able to continue with the other items on their own or in pairs.

Weaker classes: Put the grammar headings on the board and give an example of your own for each item, e.g. *I can speak English.*; *I don't like going to the cinema.*; *I'm speaking English.*; *The school is opposite the bank.*; *Can I leave the room?*

In pairs, students now match the grammar items in their book. Check answers.

Answers
can/can't for ability: Kangaroos can hop 10 metres.
like / don't like + −ing: I like watching tennis on TV.
Present continuous: I'm having my lunch.
Prepositions: The film starts at 8.30.
can/can't for permission: Can I try them on?

Use vocabulary

Write the headings on the board. Go through the items in the Student's Book and check understanding. Ask students if they can think of one more item for the *Feelings* heading. Elicit some responses and add them to the list on the board. Students now do the same for the other headings. Some possibilities are:

Feelings: *happy, sad*

Sports: *swim, play football, play basketball*

House/furniture: *sink, chair, cooker, bed, wardrobe*

Months: *November, January, February*, etc.

Clothes: *socks, shirt, skirt, dress, jacket, coat, jumper*

9 Don't close the door!

Unit overview

TOPIC: Feelings

TEXTS
Listening: to a story about a relationship; a song
Reading: a letter to a boyfriend
Reading and listening: photo story: *I miss San Francisco*
Writing: an email about friends and school

SPEAKING
Describing how you feel

LANGUAGE
Grammar: Negative imperatives
Pronunciation: Linking sounds
Vocabulary: Adjectives to describe feelings; Everyday English: *I miss*; *What's the matter?, She's/He's fine.*

1 Listen

Warm up

Ask students if they have had an argument recently. If so, who with and what about? Ask them how they felt and how the other person involved felt. This can be done in L1.

a 🔊 Give students a few minutes to look at the pictures and read the questions. Elicit their responses. Play the recording while students listen and check their answers.

TAPESCRIPT

Girl   And you know, Mum, I really don't love Martin any more and now he's not here, I'm really happy.

Mother   Oh, that's wonderful, dear. You know … Who's that?

Girl   I've got no idea. All right, all right. Hang on a minute. I'm coming. Oh, it's you! What do you want?

Martin   Don't close the door, Anna. I just want to talk to you.

Girl   Oh Martin. Go away! Leave me alone!

Martin   Anna, don't shout, please. Look – you're angry. I know that.

Girl   Angry?! Of course I'm angry! Go away – I don't want to talk to you!

Martin   I … I know … but, please … read this letter.

Girl   All right. Give it to me. Now leave me alone. Oh, no …

Answers
1 A girl, Anna, and her mother.
2 Because she doesn't want to see her boyfriend Martin.

b 🔊 Go through the example as a class. Explain that students must put the other pictures in the correct order. Give them a few minutes to complete the exercise. Play the recording while students listen and check answers.

Answers
1 e   2 b   3 a   4 c   5 f   6 d

┌── OPTIONAL ACTIVITY ─────────
Students can act out the dialogue from Exercise 1.

2 Grammar

Negative imperatives

a 🔊 Students read through sentences 1 to 4.

Stronger classes: They can do this without listening again and can listen and check only.

Weaker classes: Play the recording from Exercise 1 again for students to listen. Students match the names to the sentences.

Check answers, playing and pausing the recording again as necessary.

Answers
1 Anna   2 Martin   3 Anna   4 Martin

b Students look at the imperatives in Exercise 2a again. Elicit which ones are positive and which ones are negative and elicit the rule for each if possible at this stage. Give students a few minutes to read and complete the rule in the box.

Answer
Don't

┌── OPTIONAL ACTIVITY ─────────
To check understanding at this point, call out a few verbs, a student's name and the words positive or negative. The students must supply the positive or negative imperative of the verb. For example:

T: Juana, sit, positive.
S1: Sit!
T: Pietro, stand up, negative.
S2: Don't stand up! etc.

c Give students a few minutes to look at the pictures and the words in the box. Go through the first item as an example, if necessary. Students complete the exercise. Check answers.

Answers
2 Don't laugh.
3 Don't go away.
4 Don't cry.

(d) Students read through sentences 1 to 5 and look at signs a to e. Go through the example as a class and students find the matching sign. Students complete the exercise.

Weaker classes: This exercise can be completed in two stages: students match the sentences then check answers. Students then match the completed sentences to the signs. Check answers.

Answers
1a Don't park your car here!
2c Don't use your mobile phone!
3b Don't walk on the grass!
4e Don't open this door!
5d Don't drink the water!

> **Language note**
> Students may find it useful to translate some of these sentences into their own language to see the differences.

Grammar notebook
Remind students to note down the rules for negative imperlatives and some examples from this section in their notebooks.

┌─ OPTIONAL ACTIVITY ─────────────────

Stronger classes
They can draw their own designs and ask a partner to work out the imperative. Students could draw signs for round the classroom which could then be used.

Weaker classes
Elicit some verbs as a class and some imperative sentences. Students can then draw some signs based on those sentences.

3 Pronunciation
Linking sounds

(a) ◁)) Students read through the sentences. Play the recording while students listen. Ask students if they heard the *t* sound (no). Play the sentences again if necessary to make sure students are clear on this area.

TAPESCRIPT
Don't laugh. Don't cry. Don't shout. I don't like hamburgers.

(b) ◁)) Students read the sentences. Play the recording while students listen. Ask students if they heard the *t* sound (yes). Play the sentences again if necessary to make sure students are clear on this area. Ask them why they could hear the *t* in these sentences but not in Exercise 3a sentences and elicit or explain that it is because the *t* is before a vowel in the sentences in Exercise 3b. Play the sentences in Exercises 3a and 3b again, pausing for students to repeat.

TAPESCRIPT
Don't open the door. Don't eat that. I don't understand.

4 Vocabulary
How do you feel?
Warm up

Books closed. Elicit any adjectives for feelings students know in English and write them on the board.

(a) ◁)) Students open their books at page 66 and look at the adjectives in the box and pictures 1 to 8. Go through the first item as an example, if necessary. Students complete the exercise. Play the recording for students to listen and check answers.

TAPESCRIPT/ANSWERS
1 confused   2 worried   3 bored   4 scared
5 angry   6 happy   7 sad   8 excited

(b) ◁)) Play the recording, pausing after the first item. Go through the answer as a class, making sure students all agree.

Stronger classes: Play the recording once and then students complete the exercise. Remind them to use adjectives from Exercise 4a.

Weaker classes: Play the recording once for students to listen only, play it a second time for students to listen and write an adjective. Remind them to use adjectives from Exercise 4a.

Check answers, playing and pausing the recording again as necessary.

TAPESCRIPT
1 Stop it, will you. I said STOP!
2 Oh, no. Look! Uuuh! A snake!
3 Oh, this film. It's awful!
4 Come on, yes, shoot! Yes, GOOOOOOAL!
5 (*unhappy crying*)
6 Oh no! I've got this test tomorrow – and I don't think I know the answers ...

Answers
2 scared   3 bored   4 excited   5 unhappy
6 worried

5 Speak

Divide the class into pairs. Students read through situations 1 to 6. Check any problems. Ask a stronger pair to demonstrate the example dialogue. Students take turns to ask and answer about each situation. Monitor and check students are taking turns and that they are responding using appropriate adjectives. Ask pairs to feedback to the class about their partner.

Vocabulary notebook
Encourage students to start a section called *Adjectives of feeling* and to note down the words from this section and any translations which will help them.

6 Read

(a) Ask students *Does Anna love Martin*? Give them a few minutes to read the letter and find the answer (no).

(b) Students read through sentences 1 to 4. Check any problems.

Stronger classes: They can do this without reading the letter again and can then read and check only.

Weaker classes: Students can read the letter again. Go through the first item as an example and then students complete the exercise.

Check answers, encouraging students to correct the false answers.

Answers
1 False. She's still angry.
2 False. He still loves her and wants to be her boyfriend.
3 False. She says 'Don't visit me again. Don't write and don't call.'
4 True

7 Listen

(a) 🔊 Students read through the gapped song on page 67. Check any problems.

Stronger classes: They can predict which verbs they think go in each gap and then listen and check.

Weaker classes: Play the song once while students listen only. Give them time to complete the exercise.

Check answers, playing and pausing the song after each gap for students to clarify any problems.

TAPESCRIPT

I've got a new computer, I've got lots of CDs,
I've got everything that I need
but I haven't got you.

I've got a fancy car, and a colour TV,
I've got everything that I need
but I haven't got you.

Refrain:
Don't break my heart,
Don't tell me this is the end.
Don't shout at me,
Don't tell me you've got a new man.
Oh, baby give me one more chance.
Don't close the door, don't close the door on me.

I eat in the best restaurants.
And I sleep in top hotels.
Everyone tells me I'm great.
I've got everything that I want
but I haven't got you.

Answers
1 Don't close
2 Don't break
3 Don't tell
4 Don't shout
5 Don't tell
6 Don't close
7 don't close

(b) Divide the class into pairs. Students discuss their opinions of the song before feeding back to the class.

I miss San Francisco

8 Read and listen

If you set the background information as a homework research task, ask students to tell the rest of the class what they found out.

BACKGROUND INFORMATION

San Francisco: Is a large US city situated on the west coast of California between the Pacific Ocean and San Francisco Bay. They are connected by a strait called The Golden Gate. It is the USA's largest port on the west coast and a lot of trade is done with Asia, Alaska and Hawaii from there. The city was founded in 1776 by the Spanish and they named it Yerba Buena but it was taken and claimed by the Americans in 1846. In 1848 the California Gold Rush meant that many people came to California in search of their fortune. It is also a city which has suffered several major earthquakes.

Cambridge: See Background information in Unit 5.

a (◁)) Students read the questions. Give them a few minutes to read and listen to the story and find the answers. Check answers as a class.

Answers
She's in her bedroom, at home in Cambridge.
The woman is her mother.

b (◁)) Students read through questions 1 to 4 and the possible answers. Check any problems. Make sure students understand that only one answer is correct. Go through the first one as an example, if necessary referring students back to the story on page 68. Play the recording while students listen and read. Students complete the exercise. Check answers. Play the recording again, pausing as necessary for students to clarify any problems.

TAPESCRIPT
See the photo story on page 68 of the Student's Book.

Answers
1 b   2 a   3 b   4 a

┌─ OPTIONAL ACTIVITY ─────────────
In pairs, students can act out the dialogue in the photo story.

9 Everyday English

a Students read expressions 1 to 3 and locate who says them in the photo story. Check answers. Students then translate the expressions into their own language.

Answers
1 Amy's mum   2 Amy   3 Amy

b Students read through dialogues 1 to 3. Check any problems. Go through the first item as an example, if necessary. Students complete the exercise. Check answers.

Answers
1 miss   2 's fine   3 What's the matter

Vocabulary notebook
Students should add the expressions and translations from this section to their *Everyday English* section in their notebooks.

┌─ OPTIONAL ACTIVITY ─────────────
Stronger classes
In pairs, students write new dialogues using the expressions from Exercise 9. They can then act them out in front of the class. Encourage them to use adjectives and imperatives from this unit too.

Weaker classes
They can act out the dialogues from Exercise 9b.

10 Write

a Students read the email and answer the question.

Answer
There's a new boy called Brad in her class and a new English teacher. She's got lots of questions about school, friends and teachers.

b This task can be set for homework. Students read through the points they must include in their email reply.

Stronger classes: They can draft their emails and then write a final version for homework.

Weaker classes: Go through each point as a class and elicit examples. Students then draft their email and swap with a partner to check. They can then produce a final version.

10 We can't lose

Unit overview

TOPICS: Sporting achievements and sport in British schools

TEXTS
Reading and listening: a text about a disabled athlete
Listening: to information about abilities of people and animals
Listening: to a dialogue about sports
Reading: Culture in mind: *Sport in British schools*
Writing: replying to an email about sports you do

SPEAKING
Asking and answering about ability

LANGUAGE
Grammar: *Can/can't* (ability)
Pronunciation: *Can/can't*; *like / don't like + –ing*
Vocabulary: Sports

1 Read and listen

Warm up

Books closed. Ask students if they know anyone who has won any sporting competitions. If so, what for? If not, ask them what kind of sport they like watching live or on television. If they have watched live sport, which event did they attend?

a Give students a few minutes to look at the pictures and read the questions. Elicit suggestions but do not give answers at this stage. Pre-teach any vocabulary, e.g. *wheelchair, cerebral palsy, triathlon, take part, lie*.

Stronger classes: They can read the article silently and check their answers.

Weaker classes: Read the article aloud as a class and then ask students to check their answers.

Answers
The man in the wheelchair is Rick Hoyt and the man pushing him is his father.

b 🔊 Students read through questions 1 to 5. Check any problems. Go through the first item as an example, if necessary.

Stronger classes: They can answer the questions and then listen and check only.

Weaker classes: Play the recording while students read and listen. Students complete the exercise.

Check answers, playing and pausing the recording as necessary.

TAPESCRIPT
See reading text on page 70 of the Student's Book.

Answers
1 He uses a computer.
2 They swim four kilometres, cycle 180 kilometres and run 42 kilometres.
3 His father pushes him in his wheelchair in the running, he swims and pulls Rick in a small boat in the swimming and Rick sits in a special seat on the front of his father's bike in the cycling.
4 They take about 15 or 16 hours.
5 (Students' answers; can be in L1 if necessary.)

OPTIONAL ACTIVITY
You can give students the following True/False exercise on the reading text. Encourage students to correct the false answers.
1 Rick is Australian.
2 He works at the University of Birmingham.
3 He loves sport.
4 A triathlon winner usually finishes in about nine hours.
5 Rick and his father usually take ten hours to complete a triathlon.

Answers
1 False. He's American.
2 False. He works at the University of Boston.
3 True
4 True
5 False. They usually take 15 or 16 hours.

2 Grammar

can/can't (ability)

a **Stronger classes:** Students read through the examples from the article and translate them into their own language. Are there similarities or differences? Ask students to identify the positive (can) and negative (can't) form of the verb in each sentence. Ask students to give an example of something they can/can't do.

Weaker classes: Books closed. Write the following example sentences (or two of your own) on the board: *I can speak English. They can't speak Russian.*

Ask students to think about how they would say these sentences in their own language. Then ask them to identify the positive (can) and negative (can't) form of the verb in each sentence. Students open their books at page 71 and look at the examples from the reading text. Encourage students to give an example of their own for *can/can't* at this stage.

b Students go through the reading text and underline examples of *can/can't*. They can compare answers in pairs before a whole class check.

Answers
Rick can't run, cycle or swim ...
Rick can take part ...

(c) Students read through the table. Check any problems. Students complete the exercise. Check answers.

Answers
Negative: can't
Question: Can
Short answer negative: can't

Language notes

1 Students may produce sentences like ~~I don't know speak English~~. because of the way their own language works. Remind them of the function of *can* in English, if necessary.
2 Remind students that we never use the auxiliary verbs *do/does* with *can*.
3 *Can* is the same for all persons, singular and plural.
4 *Can/can't* are followed by the infinitive without *to*, e.g. *I can sing*. NOT ~~I can to sing~~.

(d) Students read through prompts 1 to 5. Check any problems. Go through the example as a class, drawing students' attention to the use of *but* to introduce the negative part of the sentence. Students complete the exercise. Check answers.

Answers

2 She can ride a bike but she can't swim.
3 They can learn to count but they can't learn to speak English.
4 I can use a computer but I can't draw pictures with it.
5 She can play the guitar but she can't play the violin.

Grammar notebook
Students should start a section called *can/can't* and make a note of the forms and any translations to help them.

3 Listen

Students read through statements 1 to 5. Check any problems.

Stronger classes: They can predict whether the statements are true or false and then listen and check only.

Weaker classes: Play the recording for students to listen only. Students complete the exercise.

Check answers, playing and pausing the recording again as necessary.

TAPESCRIPT

1 Camels are amazing animals. They can live for up to six months in the desert without water.
2 Did you know, the human eye can see over one million different colours.

3 Kangaroos don't run. They hop. They have very strong back legs. A kangaroo can hop ten metres in one go.
4 In the USA, a man called Mark Hogg can eat 94 worms in 30 seconds.
5 This is true. There is a man in Cuba who can dive without oxygen and can go to a depth of 162 metres.

Answers

1 False. They can live without water for six months.
2 True
3 False. They can hop ten metres.
4 True
5 True

┌── OPTIONAL ACTIVITY ──────────────

This can be set for homework.

Students can make up their own quiz based on animals, nature etc. and can write quiz questions using *can/can't*. Encourage them to research questions in encyclopaedias, the Internet and reference books. They can then ask a partner the questions and see how well they do.

---

4 Pronunciation

can/can't

(a) Play the recording while students listen. Ask a stronger student to explain the difference in the sounds in *can* and *can't*.

TAPESCRIPT

1 He can write on a computer, but he can't walk.
2 She can ride a bike, but she can't swim.
3 They can learn to count, but they can't learn to talk.
4 I can use a computer, but I can't draw pictures with it.

(b) Play the recording again, pausing while students repeat each sentence. Make sure students are pronouncing each *can/can't* correctly. Drill any problem sentences or drill *can/can't* in isolation.

(c) Students read the dialogues. Play the recording while students listen. Play it a second time, pausing for students to repeat.

TAPESCRIPT
1
Can you swim?
No, I can't.
2
Can you sing?
Yes, but not very well!

5 Speak

Look box

Before students begin Exercise 5, ask them to read through the information in the Look box. They can translate the expression in bold if it helps.

Divide the class into pairs. Students read through the words in the box and the example dialogue. Ask a stronger pair to demonstrate the example dialogue, drawing students' attention to the expression *but not very well* which they have just seen in the Look box. Students complete the exercise. Monitor and check students are taking turns to ask and answer and that they are adding two more questions of their own. Ask pairs to feedback to the class with information about their partner.

> **OPTIONAL ACTIVITY**
> If there are students who can do the things in the box in Exercise 5, ask them to give a short demonstration to the rest of the class.

6 Vocabulary

Sports

Warm up

Books closed. Ask students if they know the English word for any sports. Elicit the words they know and write them on the board. Ask students to compare those words with the words in their own language. Are there any similarities?

Students open their books at page 72 and read through the words in the box and look at the pictures in Exercise 6. Go through the first item as an example, if necessary.

Stronger classes: They can match the words in the box with the pictures.

Weaker classes: See if any of the elicited words on the board match the pictures first then students can work their way through the words in the box, matching them to the pictures.

Play the recording for students to listen and check answers.

TAPESCRIPT/ANSWERS

1 play volleyball
2 ski
3 play football
4 snowboard
5 play tennis
6 ride a horse
7 play basketball
8 do gymnastics
9 rollerblade

Vocabulary notebook

Encourage students to start a section called *Sports* and to note down any new words from this section.

> **OPTIONAL ACTIVITY**
> Whole class or small groups. Students choose a sport from this unit (or one of their own choice if it is a stronger class) and mime it to the rest of the group/class. The first student who guesses correctly takes the next turn.

7 Listen

If you set the background information as a homework research task, ask students to tell the rest of the class what they found out.

BACKGROUND INFORMATION

American football: Is a sport which developed from the English games of soccer and rugby. In American football there are two teams, each with 11 men. The pitch they play on is a specific size: 91.4m x 48.8m. Each end of the pitch has an end zone which is 9.14m deep. In the end zone there are H-shaped goal posts. The aim of the game is possession: the ball must be moved, run or passed across the opponent's goal line. This type of goal is called a touchdown and is worth six points. Blocking and tackling make American football one of the most physical sports there is and players must wear heavy protective clothing. The Super Bowl game for the League Championship is a major sporting event in the USA.

Soccer: Is also called association football or football. It is one of the world's most popular sports. Two teams of 11 players play against each other on a pitch measuring 100m by 73m. At either end of the pitch a goal is centred; this measures 7.3 metres wide and 2.4 metres high and is backed with netting. The aim of the game is to score a goal in your opponent's net by passing the ball. The ball can be kicked or moved with other parts of the body (not the hands and arms). The goalkeeper is the only player who can handle the ball. Football first appeared in the UK in the 14th century but association football rules were not drawn up until 1863. Each country has their own football leagues and the main international competition is the football world cup which takes place every four years.

a Students read through the list of sports. Check any problems.

Stronger classes: Ask students to predict which sports they think Alex and Amy will talk about and they can listen and check.

Weaker classes: Play the recording while students listen only. Students complete the exercise.

Check answers, playing and pausing the recording again as necessary. Ask students who mentioned which sport.

TAPESCRIPT

Alex Do you like sport, Amy?

Amy Oh, yeah. In San Francisco, I go rollerblading every week. I just love it. And I play tennis sometimes.

Alex Oh, tennis. Really?

Amy Oh, don't you like tennis?

Alex Well, I like watching it on TV sometimes, you know, Wimbledon and things, but I don't really like playing it myself. Squash is my sport. And football, of course.

Amy Oh, yeah. Me, too. The San Francisco 49ers, they're my favourite team. I love going to the games.

Alex Oh, right. You mean American football.

Amy Oh, yes, you're right, sorry. When you say football, you mean soccer, don't you? Do you play soccer, Alex? I mean, football?

Alex Yes, I do. There's a team at our school. We're really good. We usually win.

Amy Ah, maybe I can come and watch …

Answers
rollerblading, tennis, volleyball,
football (soccer), American football

b 🔊 Students read through statements 1 to 4. Check any problems. Go through the first item as an example, if necessary.

Stronger classes: They can answer the questions and then listen and check only.

Weaker classes: Play the recording again while students listen only. Students complete the exercise.

Check answers, playing and pausing the recording as necessary to clarify any problems.

Answers
1 False. She goes rollerblading every week.
2 False. He doesn't like playing tennis, but he enjoys watching it on TV.
3 True
4 True

OPTIONAL ACTIVITY

Ask students the following comprehension questions on the Listening text if you feel they need further practice.

1 How often does Amy go rollerblading in San Francisco?
2 How often does Amy play tennis?
3 Does Alex play tennis?
4 Who are Amy's favourite American football team?
5 Does Alex play football?

Answers
1 Every week.
2 Sometimes.
3 No but he watches it on TV.
4 The San Francisco 49ers.
5 Yes, he does.

8 Grammar

like / don't like + –ing

a **Stronger classes:** Students read through the examples. Elicit which verb form follows *like / don't like* and *love* (*–ing*) and ask students to give you an example of their own of something they like / don't like / love doing. Students then read through the table and complete the rule.

Weaker classes: Books closed. Write the following examples (or some of your own) on the board: *I like teaching English. I don't like doing homework. I love going to the cinema*. Ask students to identify which verb form follows *like / don't like* and *love* and elicit or explain that these verbs are always followed by the *–ing* form. Students then open their books at page 73 and read the examples and the table. Ask students to give an example of their own for the verbs. Students then complete the rule.

Check answers.

Answer
like, don't like, love

> **Language notes**
> 1 Some students may produce statements like ~~I am liking watching television. Television is liking to me.~~ because of the way their own language works. Remind them that these verbs are always followed by *–ing* in English and that the person is always the subject.
> 2 Remind students of the spelling rules for the *–ing* form if necessary:
> – verbs ending in a consonant, add *–ing*, e.g. *watch – watching*
> – verbs ending in *–e*, delete the *–e* and add *–ing*, e.g. *love – loving*
> – verbs ending in one consonant + one vowel + one consonant, double the final consonant and add *–ing*, e.g. *swim – swimming*

---

b Divide the class into pairs. Ask a stronger pair to demonstrate the example dialogue, drawing students' attention to the use of the *–ing* forms and the use of the time expressions from earlier in the unit.

Stronger classes: They can ask the same questions as in the example dialogue and then ask some more of their own.

Weaker classes: Elicit some questions (or prompts) they want to ask their partner (putting them on the board if necessary) and give them a few minutes to ask and answer.

Monitor and check students are taking turns to ask and answer and that they are using the correct forms of the verb in the box and are using some time expressions. Make a note of any repeated errors to go through as a class after the exercise.

Ask pairs to feedback on what they found out about their partner.

c Students read through sentences 1 to 5. Go through the example, if necessary. Students complete the exercise. Check answers.

Answers
2   She doesn't like going to the cinema.
3   Do your parents like going on holiday?
4   His brother really likes watching soccer.
5   I hate swimming in the sea.

Grammar notebook
Students should start a section called *like / don't like + –ing* and make a note of the rules and add some example sentences of their own.

Culture in mind

9 Read

If you set the background information as a homework research task, ask students to tell the rest of the class what they found out.

BACKGROUND INFORMATION

Year 11: This is the fifth year of secondary school education in Great Britain. Most schools are structured as follows: primary school: Years 1 to 6, secondary school: Years 7 to 13. In Years 10 and 11 students prepare for, and take at the end of the two years, exams called GCSEs. They can then choose to continue studying or leave school and find a job. If they continue studying they will study for AS levels in Year 12 and A levels in Year 13. A level results are important if students wish to go on to study in further education establishments.

Bournemouth: Is a town in Dorset on the south coast of England to the south west of Southampton. It is a popular seaside town and a popular holiday destination.

Droitwich: Is a town in the Midlands.

The Midlands: Is an area in the centre of the UK where the cities of Birmingham and Coventry are located.

Warm up

Pre-teach the words *winter* and *summer*. Ask students which sports they participate in and which sports they like watching live or on television. Does anyone play for a team? If so, in what sport and how often do they practise, play etc.?

a Students look at the pictures and read the words in the box. Give them a few minutes to match the words to the pictures. Check answers.

Answers
1 d   2 b   3 f   4 e   5 a   6 c

b Students read the instructions. Check any problems.

Stronger classes: They can read the text silently and complete the exercise.

Weaker classes: The text can be read aloud and then students can complete the exercise.

Check answers.

Answers
Miriam: netball, hockey, tennis, football
Jack: football, rugby, cricket, tennis

c Students read through sentences 1 to 6. Check any problems. Go through the first item as an example, if necessary. Students read the text again and complete the exercise. Students can compare answers in pairs before a whole class check.

Answers
1 Jack   2 Miriam   3 Miriam   4 Jack   5 Jack
6 Miriam

d Divide the class into pairs or small groups. Students read through the questions and the fact box and then discuss the question. Ask pairs/groups to feedback to the rest of the class. Are there any major differences in habits in Britain and the students' own country? If so, discuss these in more detail as a class.

Weaker classes: This can be discussed as a whole class.

10 Write

a Students read the question and then the email. Check answers.

Answer
Liverpool

b This exercise can be set for homework. Students read through the prompts they must include in their email. Remind them of the conventions of writing emails:
- Openings: Can be informal, e.g. Hello ..., Hi ...
- Main body: Does not need to be divided up into paragraphs
- Closings: Can be signed off informally, e.g. Write soon. Let me know what you think? Best wishes, etc.

Stronger classes: They can draft, check and write a final version for homework.

Weaker classes: They can draft their emails in class and then swap with a partner to check. They can produce their final versions for homework.

⑪ Reading on the roof!

Unit overview

TOPIC: present activities

TEXTS
Reading and listening: about present activities
Reading and listening: photo story: *I'm on my way!*
Reading and writing: a holiday postcard

SPEAKING
Describing a house

LANGUAGE
Grammar: Present continuous
Vocabulary: House and furniture; Everyday English:
*Come round to my place.; I'm on my way.; What are
you up to?; See you.*
Pronunciation: /h/ have

1 Read and listen

Warm up

Ask students what kinds of holidays they like going on. Have any of them ever been on a canal holiday? If so, where? Did they enjoy it? If not, would they like to go on one? This can be discussed in L1.

(a) Students look at the pictures and read the questions. Check any problems. Elicit suggestions. Pre-teach any vocabulary before students read the dialogue, e.g. *roof, sunny, play cards, babysit.*

Stronger classes: They read the dialogue and check their answers.

Weaker classes: Ask students to read the dialogue aloud to the class while students check their answers.

Did students predict correctly?

Answers
1 She is on the roof of a canal boat. She is happy because she is on holiday.
2 He is in the garden. He is babysitting and he hates babysitting.

(b) 🔊 Students read through the names 1 to 5 and the sentence endings a to e. Check any problems. Go through the example as a class.

Stronger classes: They can match the people and then listen and check only.

Weaker classes: Play the recording while students read and listen only. Students complete the exercise. Check answers, playing and pausing the recording again as necessary to clarify any problems.

TAPESCRIPT
See dialogue on page 76 of the Student's Book.

Answers
2 e   3 b   4 a   5 d

┌─ **OPTIONAL ACTIVITY** ─────────────

If you feel students need more comprehension practice, give them the following True/False exercise on the dialogue. Encourage them to correct the false answers.

1 Kate is on the beach.
2 Kate is on holiday.
3 The boat has three bedrooms.
4 Ben is at school.
5 Ben is unhappy.

Answers
1 False. She is on a canal boat.
2 True
3 False. It has two bedrooms.
4 False. He's in the garden.
5 True

2 Grammar
Present continuous

(a) **Stronger classes:** Students read through the examples from the text. Then they read the dialogue again on page 76 and underline further examples. Ask them what they notice about how the present continuous tense is formed and elicit that it is formed with the present tense of the verb *be* and the *–ing* form of the verb. At this point, elicit the negative, question and short answer forms. Students then read through and complete the table. Check answers before students complete the rule. Then ask students to give you an example of their own using the present continuous, making sure they are clear that the tense is used to talk about something happening at the time of speaking.

Weaker classes: Books closed. Write the following examples (or some of your own) on the board: *I am speaking English. You are sitting in Class 10.* Ask students to work out how the present continuous is formed and elicit or explain that it is formed using the verb *be* present tense and then the *–ing* form of the following verb. Students now open their books at page 77 and look at the examples from the dialogue. They then go through the dialogue and underline further examples of this tense. Elicit the other forms of the tense at this point and then students complete the table and the rule.

Answers
Positive: 're; 's
Negative: –ing; aren't/–ing; isn't/–ing
Question: Am/–ing; Are/–ing; Is/–ing
Short answer: am/'m not; are; aren't; is; isn't

Rule: present continuous

Look box

Draw students' attention to the verbs in the box and explain that some verbs have a spelling change in the –*ing* form. Give them the following rules:

1 Verbs which end in an –*e* in the base form: drop the –*e* and add –*ing*
2 Verbs of one or two syllables which end in a vowel plus a consonant: double the final consonant and add –*ing*

OPTIONAL ACTIVITY

Give students the following base forms and ask them to spell out the –*ing* form based on the spelling rules you gave them in the Look box:

1 travel – travelling
2 write – writing
3 eat – eating
4 drop – dropping
5 see – seeing

(b) Students read the dialogues. Check any problems. Go through the first exchange as an example, making sure students are clear about the use and form of the present continuous. Students complete the exercise. Remind them to use short forms.

Weaker classes: Put the base forms of the verbs in Exercise 2b on the board and elicit the present continuous forms. Students then use these to help them complete the exercise.

Check answers. Clarify any spelling problems.

Answers

2 's having   3 's playing   4 'm having   5 'm buying

(c) Students read through prompts 1 to 4. Go through the example as a class, drawing students' attention to the short answer and the explanation following the short answer. Students complete the exercise. Remind them to think carefully about the spelling of each verb. Check answers.

Answers

2 Are they eating ice creams? No, they aren't. They're drinking milkshakes.
3 Is she reading a book? No, she isn't. She's listening to a CD.
4 Is your father working today? No, he isn't. He's having a day off.

Grammar notebook

Encourage students to make a note of the rule and some examples and translations of their own.

OPTIONAL ACTIVITY

Whole class or small groups. Students can choose an activity from Exercise 2 (or one of their own choice if they are a stronger class) and mime it to the rest of the class/group. The others must guess what they are doing, using the present continuous tense. The student who guesses correctly takes the next turn.

3 Listen

◁)) Play the recording, pausing after the first item. Go through the example as a class, explaining to students that they must write a present continuous sentence to describe what they think the person on the recording is doing. Play the rest of the recording while students listen. If necessary, play the recording again. Check answers.

Answers

2 He's having a shower.
3 They're playing football.
4 She's swimming.
5 He's getting dressed.
6 They're singing.

4 Speak and write

(a) Give students a few minutes to look at the pictures and, in their notebooks, write present continuous sentences about the people. Remind them about spelling rules for –*ing* forms if necessary.

Do not check answers at this stage.

Divide the class into pairs. Students read their sentences to each other and see if they are both the same or if they have written different sentences. Ask pairs to feedback to the class. Does everyone agree on the sentences?

(b) Ask a stronger pair to demonstrate the example dialogue. Students now cover the sentences they wrote in Exercise 4a and ask and answer about the pictures. Monitor and check students are taking turns to ask and answer and that they are using the correct present continuous forms. Make a note of any repeated errors to go through as a class after the exercise.

(c) Students can work in the same pairs as Exercise 4b or with a different partner. Ask a stronger pair to demonstrate the example dialogue, drawing students' attention to the use of the present continuous forms and the use of *I think*. Students ask and answer about their family. Monitor and check students are taking turns to ask and answer and that they are using the correct present continuous forms. Make a note of any repeated errors to go through as a class after the exercise. Ask a few pairs to feedback to the rest of the class.

5 Pronunciation

/h/ have

🔊 Play the recording while students listen only. Play the recording again, pausing after each sentence for students to repeat. Make sure students are pronouncing the /h/ sound correctly. If there are still problems, drill a few words in isolation.

TAPESCRIPT
1 Hi! Can I help you?
2 He can walk on his hands.
3 Are you hungry? Have a hamburger.
4 Henry's having a holiday in Holland.

6 Vocabulary

House and furniture

Warm up

Books closed. Pre-teach the words *room* and *furniture,* then ask students if they know the names of any rooms in a house or pieces of furniture in English. Elicit the words they know and write them on the board (or ask students to come out and write them).

🔊 Students open their books at page 79 and look at the picture and the words in the boxes. If they have given any of the words already in the *Warm up* they can fill those in. Go through the example as a class, if necessary. Students then match the other words. Play the recording while students listen and check answers.

TAPESCRIPT/ANSWERS
1 kitchen   2 bathroom   3 bedroom   4 living room   5 hall   6 garden

a window   b door   c bed   d sofa   e chairs
f armchair   g table   h toilet   i shower   j bath
k fridge   l cooker

Vocabulary notebook
Encourage students to start a section called *House and furniture* and to note down any new words from this section and to illustrate or write translations to help them remember the new items.

Look box
Students look at the pictures and the words in the Look box. Give them a few examples round the class asking them to say where things are, using the three prepositions they have just seen. For example:
T: Bea, where is your bag?
S1: It's under my desk. etc.

7 Speak

Divide the class into pairs. Ask a stronger student to read out the example sentences, drawing students' attention to the use of the house and furniture vocabulary and the prepositions. Give students time to ask and answer about their houses/flats. Monitor and check students are taking turns to describe where they live and make a note of any repeated errors in vocabulary or pronunciation to go over as a class after the exercise. Ask pairs to feedback about their partner's house/flat.

┌─ OPTIONAL ACTIVITY ─────────────
Students work in pairs. Students can draw a plan of their own bedroom for a partner. The partner must guess using furniture vocabulary and prepositions where the furniture is in the bedroom.

I'm on my way!

8 Read and listen

(a) 🔊 Students read the questions. Accept suggestions for answers but do not give the answers at this stage. Play the recording while students read and listen and check their answers.

TAPESCRIPT
See the photo story on page 80 of the Student's Book.

Answers
1 She is at home.
2 She is in Alex's living room.

(b) Students read through questions 1 to 3. Check any problems.

Stronger classes: They can answer the questions and then read and listen to check only.

Weaker classes: Play the recording again. Students complete the exercise. Play the recording again, pausing as necessary to clarify any problems.

Answers
1 She's writing some emails (and talking to Alex on the phone).
2 They're playing Air Football.
3 Because she doesn't like Air Football.

┌─ OPTIONAL ACTIVITY ─────────────
In small groups, students can act out the dialogue from the photo story.

9 Everyday English

(a) Students read through expressions 1 to 4. Go through the first item as an example, if necessary. Students complete the exercise. Discuss how these expressions are said in the students' own language as a class.

Answers
1 Alex   2 Lucy   3 Lucy   4 Lucy

b Students read through dialogues 1 and 2. Check any problems. Go through the first item as an example if necessary showing students how only one option is possible. Students complete the exercise. They can compare answers in pairs before a whole class check.

Answers
1 Come round to my place; I'm on my way
2 What are you up to; see you

OPTIONAL ACTIVITY

Stronger classes: They can write and act out new dialogues using the expressions from Exercise 9a.

Weaker classes: In pairs, they can act out the dialogues from Exercise 9b.

10 Write

You may want to bring in blank postcards for students to do this exercise.

Warm up

Ask students if they send postcards to people when they go on holiday. If so, who do they send them to and what sort of news do they write on postcards?

Look box

Students look at the pictures and the words in the Look box. Ask a question about today. For example:

T: Janek, what's the weather like today?
S: It's sunny.

a Students read through questions 1 to 5. Check any problems. Students then read the postcard and answer the questions. Go through the first item as an example, if necessary. Check answers.

Answers
1 It's near the beach.
2 Because it's got a swimming pool.
3 They're doing some shopping in town.
4 She's having breakfast.
5 It's fantastic, sunny and warm.

b This part of the exercise can be set for homework. Students read through the questions. Check any problems. Elicit or explain the conventions of postcard writing:
- Layout: Always write on the left-hand side and put the address on the right
- Opening: This can be quite informal, e.g. Hello, Hi or Dear can be used
- Main body of letter: Complete sentences do not have to be used and it does not have to be divided up into paragraphs
- Closing: Informal signing off: Love, See you soon, Hope you're okay, etc.

Students then choose a holiday destination and imagine what they will tell their penfriend.

Stronger students: They can draft and write their final versions.

Weaker classes: Go through a draft postcard on the board. Students then draft their own versions and check them with a partner. They can produce their final versions for homework.

OPTIONAL ACTIVITY

If you have provided blank postcards for students they could illustrate the fronts or stick photos or pictures from magazines. The class could vote for the best postcard. All the postcards could be displayed round the class.

12 Can I try them on?

Unit overview

TOPIC: Clothes and shopping

TEXTS
Reading and listening: festivals around the world
Listening: shopping dialogues
Reading: Culture in mind: *London's carnival*
Writing: replying to an email about a festival in your country

SPEAKING
Asking and answering about clothes and shopping

LANGUAGE
Vocabulary: Months of the year and seasons; Clothes
Grammar: Prepositions: *at*, *in*, *on*; Asking for permission: *Can I ...? / Yes, you can. / Sorry, you can't.*; *one/ones*
Pronunciation: /æ/ and /e/

1 Read and listen

If you set the background information as a homework research task, ask students to tell the rest of the class what they found out.

BACKGROUND INFORMATION

St Patrick's Day: Is celebrated in many places around the world on March 17th. It is particularly celebrated in Ireland (where St Patrick is said to have spent a large part of his life) and in the USA.

Mardi Gras: This is traditionally the last Tuesday before the Christian fasting season of Lent. It literally means 'Fat Tuesday' and in Christian tradition people would eat lots before the fasting period of Lent began. In Great Britain it is now called 'Shrove' or 'Pancake Tuesday'. Carnivals are held in many places around the world often in the week leading up to Mardi Gras. New Orleans, Venice and Rio de Janeiro are some of the more famous ones.

Thanksgiving: Is a national holiday in the USA. It commemorates the harvest reaped by the Plymouth Colony in 1621. The first Thanksgiving Day took place on November 26th 1789. Thanksgiving always falls on the fourth Thursday of November. Turkey and pumpkin pie are popular foods eaten at this time.

New York: Is one of the US states on the east coast. It is also one of the largest cities in the USA.

Chicago: Is a US city in the state of Illinois. It is the third largest US city and is situated on Lake Michigan. It has some of the world's tallest skyscrapers, The Sears Tower and the John Hancock Tower.

Baltimore: Is a US city in North Maryland, set on the Patapsco River estuary. It is one of the ten largest US cities and is a major seaport.

New Orleans: Is a US city in south east Louisiana between the Mississippi river and Lake Pontchartrain. It is one of the largest and most important US cities in the south of the country. It is a very cosmopolitan city with French influences in its Creole culture. It is famous for its Mardi Gras festival and its jazz music.

Warm up

Ask students if they have any special festivals in their city/country. Ask students when the festivals are celebrated and to describe what happens during the festivals. This can be done in L1 if necessary.

(a) Elicit the names of any American festivals students know already. Students then look at the pictures on page 82 and match the photos to the names of the three festivals listed in the article. Students read the text quickly and check answers.

Weaker classes: You may want to pre-teach some vocabulary, e.g. *parade, scarf, sweater, skirt, trousers, jazz, carnival, colourful, balloons, pumpkin.*

Answers
1 St Patrick's Day = Photo b
2 Mardi Gras = Photo c
3 Thanksgiving = Photo a

(b) 🔊 Students read through sentences 1 to 3. Check any problems. Play the recording while students read and listen. Go through the first item as an example, if necessary. Students complete the exercise. Check answers, playing and pausing the recording again as necessary.

TAPESCRIPT
See reading text on page 82 of the Student's Book.

Answers
1 St Patrick's Day and Mardi Gras
2 Thanksgiving
3 Mardi Gras

OPTIONAL ACTIVITY
In pairs or small groups, students can choose which festival they would like to go to and the reasons why. They can then feedback to the rest of the class.

Alternatively, you can give them this True/False exercise based on the reading text. Encourage students to correct the false answers.

1 St Patrick's Day is in February.
2 St Patrick's Day is important for English Americans.
3 Mardi Gras takes place in New Orleans.
4 Mardi Gras lasts for three weeks.
5 Thanksgiving takes place on the last Thursday in November.
6 People eat turkey and pumpkin at Thanksgiving.

Answers
1 False. It's in March.
2 False. Irish Americans.
3 True
4 False. It lasts for two weeks.
5 True
6 True

2 Vocabulary
Months of the year and seasons
Warm up

Stronger classes: Books closed. Write the date in full on the board and draw students' attention to the month. Elicit any other months of the year they may know in English and put them on the board.

You can ask a few students to come out and try to put the months in order at this stage if students have come up with a significant number.

Weaker classes: Put all the months on the board in English in jumbled order. Ask students to come out and write them in the correct order.

(a) (🔊) Students open their books at page 83 and look at the months in Exercise 2a. Students read through the months quickly.

Stronger classes: Play the recording while students listen and underline the main stress.

Weaker classes: It may be useful to write all the months on the board before you play the recording if you did not do this in the *Warm up*. Play the recording, pausing after January. Elicit where the stress falls and mark it on the board, as in the example. Play the rest of the recording while students listen and underline the stress.

Play the recording for students to check their answers, pausing as necessary to clarify any problems.

TAPESCRIPT
January   February   March   April   May   June
July   August   September   October   November
December

(b) Students go back through the text on page 82 and underline any months in it. Check answers.

Answers
St Patrick's Day text: March
Mardi Gras: February, March
Thanksgiving: November

Vocabulary notebook
Encourage students to start a section called *Months of the year* and to note down the months from this section.

─── OPTIONAL ACTIVITY ───

Stronger classes: In pairs, students can discuss what their favourite month is and why, e.g. the month their birthday falls in, the month they have holidays, etc.

Weaker classes: Call out a student's name and give them a month of the year in random order. The student then supplies you with the month which follows. Continue in this way until all 12 months have been practised. For example:

T: Laura, August.
S1: September. Marc.
S2: October. etc.

(c) (🔊) Students read through the words in the box. Check students know how to pronounce each season: /ˈsʌməʳ/ /ˈɔːtəm/ /ˈwɪntəʳ/ /sprɪŋ/. Go through the first item as a class, if necessary. Students complete the exercise. Play the recording once for students to listen and check. Play the recording a second time, pausing for students to repeat.

TAPESCRIPT/ANSWERS
1a summer   2d autumn   3c spring   4b winter

(d) Divide the class into pairs. Give students a few minutes to discuss the questions and then feedback to the class.

Language note
Students may find it useful to compare how the seasons are said in their own language and how they are said in English.

Vocabulary notebook
Encourage students to make a note of the seasons in English.

3 Grammar and speaking
Prepositions

(a) Students read through the examples in the table. Ask students if they can see any patterns in when we use each preposition and elicit that *at* is usually used with times, *in* with months and seasons and *on* with days of the week. To check understanding at this point, ask a few students to give you some examples of their own using the prepositions from the table.

(b) Students read through sentences 1 to 4. Check any problems. Go through the first item as an example, if necessary. Students complete the exercise. Check answers.

Answers
1 at   2 on   3 in   4 in

(c) Divide the class into pairs. Ask a stronger student to read out the example sentences, drawing students' attention to the preposition in each. Ask students to explain why each preposition is used to make sure they understand. Students exchange information about themselves. Monitor and check students are taking turns to give information and that they are using the correct prepositions and the correct pronunciation of the months of the year. Ask a few pairs to feedback to the rest of the class.

Grammar notebook
Encourage students to copy the table from Exercise 3a into their notebook and to write translations if necessary.

┌─ OPTIONAL ACTIVITY ─────────────
Whole class. Call out a time, season or month and a student's name. The student must supply you with the correct preposition to go with the word you have called out. Continue in this way until you feel students are clear about which prepositions go with which words.

4 Vocabulary
Clothes

(a) Books closed. Elicit the names of any clothes students know already in English and write them on the board. Check students know how to pronounce each word. Students then open their books at page 84 and look at the picture of the clothes. They match the names of the clothes from the box with the picture. Go through the first item as an example if necessary. Then play the recording while students listen and check. Play the recording a second time, pausing after each item for students to repeat.

TAPESCRIPT/ANSWERS
1 e T shirt   2 f scarf   3 c shirt   4 a dress
5 g trousers   6 i jumper   7 h socks   8 j jacket
9 d top   10 b jeans   11 k shoes   12 l trainers

(b) Students go back through the text on page 82 and underline examples of clothes. They can compare answers in pairs before a whole class check.

Answers
St Patrick's Day: hats, scarves, sweaters, skirts, trousers

Language notes
1 Remind students that we use the verb *wear* with clothes in English.
2 The word *trousers* is always plural in English.

Vocabulary notebook
Encourage students to start a section called *Clothes* and to note down the words for clothes from this section and illustrate or translate the items to help remember them.

┌─ OPTIONAL ACTIVITY ─────────────
Pairs. Students take a few minutes to look at what their partner is wearing. They then stand back to back and describe the clothes and the colours of each item to the rest of the class. The rest of the class must decide if the student has given an accurate description of their partner.

5 Listen

Students look at the pictures.

Stronger classes: Play the recording while students listen and write in the correct order.

Weaker classes: Elicit and write on the board what each model is wearing so students know what they are listening for. Play the recording, pausing after the first item and go through this as an example. Play the rest of the recording while students listen and mark the order. Check answers. Play the recording again to clarify any problems, if necessary.

TAPESCRIPT
1
OK, and here comes our first model, Jonathan. He's looking great in his blue jeans, his grey trainers and his white T-shirt. And what a lovely leather jacket too! Let's give him a big hand.

2
And here comes Samantha. Isn't she elegant in her blue dress, black shoes and her wonderful white scarf? Thank you very much, Samantha. And can I ask for a round of applause for our Samantha, please.

3
And now, George. Well, how do you like these grey trousers, with the green shirt and the black jumper? Isn't that a beautiful combination? A big hand for George, please. Thank you.

4
All right, and here we have Sylvia. And Sylvia's wearing a grey skirt with a pink top and beautiful black shoes. Let's give her a big hand too.

Answers
a 2   b 4   c 1   d 3

6 Speak

a Divide the class into pairs. Ask a stronger pair to
read out the example dialogue. Students exchange
information in their pairs. Remind them to choose
characters from different pages and not to show their
partner which page they are looking at. Monitor and
check students are taking turns to ask and answer.

b Students can work with the same partner from
Exercise 6a or swap pairs so they have a new partner.
Give students a few minutes to read through the
prompt questions. Check any problems. Ask a stronger
pair to demonstrate the answer to the first question.
Give students a few minutes to ask and answer.
Monitor and check students are taking turns to ask
and answer and that they are answering appropriately.

7 Pronunciation

/æ/ and /e/

a 🔊 Students read the words in each column. Play
the recording, pausing after each word for students
to repeat.

TAPESCRIPT
/æ/ black   jacket   hamburger   thanks   January
/e/ yes   red   dress   yellow   September

b 🔊 Students read sentences 1 to 3 silently. Drill
each sentence as a class, focusing particularly on
the /æ/ and /e/ sounds. If you feel students are still
having problems, drill a few words from Exercise 7a
in isolation. Play the recording, pausing after each
sentence for students to repeat.

TAPESCRIPT
1 I like the black jacket in the window.
2 I wear red in January and yellow in September.
3 She's wearing a black and red dress.

8 Grammar

can/can't (asking for permission)

a Students read the question and then the two
dialogues and find the answer.

Weaker classes: You may want to read the dialogues
aloud as a class.

Answer
Dialogue 1: He wants to buy trainers.
Dialogue 2: She wants to buy a shirt.

b Students read the example.

Stronger classes: Elicit when the expression is used.

Weaker classes: They may find it helpful to refer
back to the dialogues in Exercise 8a and locate the
expression in each. Then they can explain when it
is used.

Answer
When someone is asking for permission to do or
have something.

c Students now go back through the dialogue in
Exercise 8a and underline examples of the expression.

Weaker classes: If you have already located the
expressions in Exercise 8b students can underline
them now.

Answers
Dialogue 1: Can I try them on?
Dialogue 2: Can I have that green shirt please?

d 🔊 Students look at the pictures. Play the
recording, pausing after the first dialogue and go
through this as an example. Play the rest of the
recording while students listen and match. Students
can compare answers in pairs before a whole class
check.

TAPESCRIPT
1
Boy   Can I use your stereo?
Girl   I'm sorry, James. I'm using it.
Boy   OK.

2
Girl   Is that book good?
Boy   Yes, it's great.
Girl   Can I read it?
Boy   Yes, of course you can! Here you are!

3
Man   Can I try this shirt on, please?
Woman Yes, of course.

4
Girl   Dad, can I watch my programme now?
Man   No, sorry, you can't. I'm watching the
         football.

Answers
1 c 2 d 3 a 4 b

(e) 🔊 Students read through dialogues 1 and 2.

Stronger classes: They can predict the missing words and then listen and check only.

Weaker classes: Play the recording while students listen only. Give students time to fill in the gaps.

Check answers, playing and pausing the recording as necessary to clarify any problems.

Play the recording again, pausing after each dialogue for long enough for students to repeat.

TAPESCRIPT
See dialogues 1 and 2 for Exercise 8d.

Answers
Dialogue 1: Can; I'm sorry
Dialogue 2: Can; Yes, of course you can

┌─ OPTIONAL ACTIVITY ─────────

Weaker classes: Ask pairs to act out the dialogues from Exercise 8e.

(f) Divide the class into pairs. Students look at the pictures. Ask a stronger pair to demonstrate an example dialogue for the first picture. Remind them to use expressions with *Can I ...?* etc. Students complete the dialogues for each picture. Monitor and check students are taking turns to ask and answer and that they are using appropriate expressions for each picture. Ask pairs to read out or act out their dialogues to the rest of the class.

Suggested answers
Can I borrow your bike, please? Yes, of course you can. / No, sorry, you can't.
Can I try on those shoes, please? Yes, certainly. What size?
Can I have an ice cream, please? Yes, OK. / Sorry, you can't.
Can I watch TV now? Yes, all right. / No, not now.

one/ones

(g) Students read through the examples.

Stronger classes: Elicit or explain when *one/ones* is used (*one* is used to replace a singular countable noun that has already been mentioned; *ones* replaces a plural countable noun that has already been mentioned).

Weaker classes: Ask them to look at each sentence and to find a noun in the first part (*trainers/shirt*). Ask them what they can tell you about each noun and elicit that *trainers* is plural and countable and *shirt* is singular and countable. Follow the Stronger classes procedure from this point.

(h) Students read through the two dialogues. Go through the example as a class, drawing students' attention to the noun which *ones* replaces (*trousers*). Students

complete the exercise. Students can compare answers in pairs before a whole class check.

Answers
1 ones
2 one; one; one

┌─ OPTIONAL ACTIVITY ─────────
Stronger classes
They can write and act out their own dialogues asking and giving permission and including *one/ones*.

Weaker classes
They can act out their completed dialogues from Exercise 8h.

Culture in mind

9 Read

If you set the background information as a homework research task, ask students to tell the rest of the class what they found out.

BACKGROUND INFORMATION

London: See Background information in Unit 5.

Notting Hill carnival: Takes place in the area of Ladbroke Grove in London every August. It has been held during the August bank holiday weekend since 1966. The festivities started as a local affair set up by the West Indian immigrants, particularly those from Trinidad and it has now become a full Caribbean Carnival with floats, stalls, steel drum bands, etc. Over 2 million people attend the carnival each year.

Mas parade: Is a parade in a carnival where people dress up. Mas is short for masquerade.

Calypso music: Is a style of Afro-Caribbean music which originated in the British/French colonial islands of the Caribbean at the start of the twentieth century. Trinidad was an important centre of early calypso; other famous artists come from Jamaica and the West Indies. It is a very popular style of music at West Indian carnival celebrations.

Trinidad and Tobago: Are two islands in the West Indies to the north of Venezuela. The capital is Port of Spain which is on the island of Trinidad. Trinidad was discovered by Christopher Columbus in 1498 but was given to the British in 1815. Tobago, which was originally held by the French and Dutch, became British in the late 1700s. The islands were joined politically in 1888. In 1962 they became an independent state.

Warm up

Books closed. Ask students if they have heard of the Notting Hill carnival. Ask them where they think it takes place (London) and when (in August) and elicit responses. Students then open their books at page 86 and read the text quickly and find the answers.

(a) Pre-teach any vocabulary, e.g. *floats, costumes, steel bands, stalls*. Students read through items 1 to 5. Check any problems. Give students a few minutes to match them to the pictures. If necessary, do the first item as an example. Check answers.

Answers

1 d 2 b 3 e 4 a 5 c

(b) Students read through questions 1 to 5. Go through the first item as an example, if necessary. Give students time to read the text again and answer the questions. Check answers.

Answers

1 Nearly two million.
2 More than forty years old.
3 It lasts for two days.
4 It is a huge carnival parade.
5 Calypso.

(c) Divide the class into pairs or small groups. Give students time to discuss the questions and then ask them to feedback to the class.

10 Write

If you set the background information as a homework research task, ask students to tell the rest of the class what they found out.

BACKGROUND INFORMATION

Halloween: Is traditionally celebrated on October 31st, the eve of All Saints' Day. The name was originally known in medieval England as All Hallows. Children nowadays dress up and go round houses in their neighbourhood asking for treats and if they don't receive a treat they may play a trick on the person.

Trick or Treat: This is what children ask neighbours for on Halloween. Treats can be sweets or money. If people did not provide a treat then children could play a trick on the person. It was originally an American custom but one which is becoming more popular in the UK.

Warm up

Ask students to look at the pictures and suggest what this festival is called and when this festival happens.

(a) Pre-teach any vocabulary, e.g. *witches, ghosts*. Students read the question. Give them a few minutes to read the email to check their predictions to the *Warm up* and to find the answer.

Answers

Young people knock on people's doors and get treats, or they play tricks on people who don't give them treats.

(b) This exercise can be set for homework. Students read the prompt questions.

Stronger classes: They can draft their own answers to the questions and make their own notes. They can then write a final version, checking that they have answered all the questions.

Weaker classes: Go through each question as a class, eliciting and putting the suggestions on the board. Students can then use the information on the board to draft their email. They can then swap with a partner and check the drafts before producing their final version.

OPTIONAL ACTIVITY

Students can bring in photos or illustrate their emails with pictures of the festivals they have written about.

Module 3 **Check your progress**

1 **Grammar**

(a)
2 Do you like watching soaps on TV?
3 My brother likes swimming in the sea.
4 Her cat doesn't like drinking milk.

(b)
2 can stand on his head, he can walk on his hands
3 can play football, she can't rollerblade
4 can't sing, they can dance

(c)
2 Can, try on 3 Can, open 4 Can, play
5 Can, borrow

(d)
1 I'm reading a book.
2 She's having a shower.
3 They're watching TV.
4 He's looking for a CD.

(e) 1 one 2 ones 3 ones

(f) 1 at 2 on 3 at 4 in

(g) 2 Come 3 Don't watch 4 Write

2 **Vocabulary**

(a) Months: June, August, April
Seasons: summer, winter, autumn

(b) 2 trousers 3 scarf 4 dress 5 jumper
6 socks 7 trainers 8 hat 9 jacket

(c) 2 fridge 3 living room 4 table 5 bathroom
6 shower 7 sofa 8 bedroom 9 cooker

(d) 2 angry 3 excited 4 bored 5 unhappy

3 **Everyday English**

2 I miss her
3 what are you up to
4 Come round to my place
5 I'm on my way
6 See you

How did you do?
Check that students are marking their scores. Collect these in and check them as necessary and discuss any further work needed with specific students.

Module 4
Past and present

YOU WILL LEARN ABOUT ...

Ask students to look at the photos on the page and to read through the topics in the box. Check any problems. In small groups, students discuss which topic area they think each photo matches.

Answers
1 The Beatles
2 A chef from Scotland
3 A famous nurse
4 Holiday camps in Britain
5 The *Mary Celeste* mystery
6 John Lennon
7 Lord Lucan
8 A South African hero

YOU WILL LEARN HOW TO ...

See Introduction.

Use grammar

Go through the example as a class.

Stronger classes: Should be able to continue with the other items on their own or in pairs.

Weaker classes: Put the grammar headings on the board and give an example of your own for each item, e.g. *I was 25 on my birthday. We were in Scotland last summer. I watched TV last night. I saw you in town yesterday. Juan is taller than Luisa.*

In pairs, students now match the grammar items in their book. Check answers.

Answers
Past simple *were/weren't*: They were in New York.
Past simple regular verbs: She wanted to be a nurse.
Past simple irregular verbs: No one knew where he went.
Comparative adjectives: Delhi is hotter than London.

Use vocabulary

Write the headings on the board. Go through the items in the Student's Book and check understanding. Ask students if they can think of one more item for the *Time expressions* heading. Elicit some responses and add them to the list on the board. Students now do the same for the other headings. Some possibilities are:

Time expressions: *last year, this morning, two weeks ago, last summer*

Adverbs: *quietly, suddenly, carefully, angrily*

Adjectives: *good, bad, young, old, easy, difficult*

13 He was only 40

Unit overview

TOPIC: The death of John Lennon

TEXTS
Reading and listening: an article about the death of John Lennon
Listening: to a dialogue about the Beatles; to dates
Reading and listening: photo story: *Rob's wallet*
Writing: an email to a friend about a holiday

SPEAKING
Asking and answering using time expressions
Talking about past situations; dates

LANGUAGE
Grammar: Past simple: *was/wasn't*; *were/weren't*
Pronunciation: *was/wasn't* and *were/weren't*
Vocabulary: Time expressions; Ordinal numbers and dates; Everyday English: *Calm down!*; *Can I have a look?*; *Oh, brilliant!*; *You must be joking!*

1 Read and listen

If you set the background information as a homework research task, ask students to tell the rest of the class what they found out.

BACKGROUND INFORMATION

John Lennon: Was born on 9th October 1940 in Liverpool. He was a rhythm guitarist, a keyboard player and a vocalist. He met the musician Paul McCartney in 1957 and they formed the Beatles in 1960. In 1962, Lennon married Cynthia Powell and they had a son, John Julian Lennon. They divorced in 1968. In 1969 he met and married the Japanese conceptual artist and musician, Yoko Ono. They had a son, Sean Lennon, in 1975. John Lennon was murdered in October 1980. Liverpool airport has been renamed John Lennon International airport after him.

The Beatles: The English rock group of the 1960s who are said to influence music to this day. The group were from Liverpool and were John Lennon (1940–1980), Paul McCartney (1942–), George Harrison (1943–2002) and Ringo Starr (Richard Starkey) (1940–). Lennon and McCartney wrote most of the songs and music. The group had their first number one hit single in 1963 with the song *Please Please Me* and they went on to have many more hits.

By 1966 they had had eight more number one singles and five number one albums. Paul McCartney went on to form his own pop group *Wings* in 1971 after the Beatles split up.

Mark Chapman: Was born in 1955 and was a security guard from Hawaii. He shot and killed John Lennon in October 1980.

Yoko Ono: Was born in 1933 in Tokyo. In 1957 she married a Japanese composer, Toshi Ichiyanagi. In 1964 she divorced him and married Tony Cox; she then went on to marry John Lennon. She now works to promote peace through the John Lennon Foundation and markets children's toys under the John Lennon brand.

Warm up

Ask students if they know the date (or the year) John Lennon was killed (8 December 1980). Put suggestions on the board.

(a) Students read the questions and look at the pictures. Elicit suggestions. Students then read the article quickly and check their answers and their *Warm up* predictions.

Weaker classes: You may want to pre-teach some vocabulary, e.g. *recording studio*, *autograph*, *apartment*, *shots*.

Answers
The men are John Lennon and Mark Chapman. John Lennon was a member of the popular group the Beatles and Mark Chapman was the person who shot John Lennon.

(b) 🔊 Students quickly read through statements 1 to 4. Check any problems. Go through the first item as an example, if necessary.

Stronger classes: They can complete the exercise and listen and check only.

Weaker classes: Play the recording once while students listen and read. Students complete the exercise. Play the recording again, pausing after each answer for students to check answers. Encourage students to correct the false answers.

TAPESCRIPT
See reading text on page 92 of the Student's Book.

Answers
1 True
2 False. He was American.
3 False. There were five shots.
4 False. They were there in three minutes.

2 Grammar

Past simple: *was/wasn't* and *were/weren't*

a **Stronger classes:** Students read through the examples from the reading text. Elicit which verbs are singular (*was/wasn't*) and which plural (*were*). Also elicit how the negative is formed (*was + not*). Ask them to give you an example using the negative plural form. Ask a few students to volunteer examples of their own using the different forms. Students then read and complete the table.

Weaker classes: Books closed. Write the following examples (or some of your own) on the board: *You were in Class X last year. I was in Scotland last summer. John Lennon wasn't a member of the Rolling Stones.* Ask them to identify which are the singular (*was*) and plural forms (*were*), and negative (*wasn't*). Then ask them to work out how the negative plural form is made (*were + not*). Ask a few students to give you an example of their own using *was/wasn't* or *were/weren't*. Students open their books at page 93 and look at the examples from the reading text. Give them a few minutes to complete the table.

Answers
Positive: was
Negative: was not; weren't
Question: Were
Short answer: wasn't

b Students quickly look through the text again and underline all the other examples of the verb *be*.

c Students read through questions 1 to 7. Go through the example as a class, if necessary. Students complete the exercise. Check answers.

Answers
2 Were   3 Was   4 Were   5 Was   6 Was   7 Was

> **Language note**
> Remind students that both the first and third person singular form is *was* and all other persons use *were*. We say *You were* NOT ~~You was~~.

Grammar notebook
Remind students to start a section called *Past simple: was/were* and *were/weren't* and to note down the completed table and some examples of their own from this exercise.

3 Pronunciation

was/wasn't and *were/weren't*

a 🔊 Students read sentences 1 to 4. Play the recording, pausing after each sentence for students to repeat.

TAPESCRIPT
1   He was only 40.
2   They were in New York.
3   There wasn't a pen in his hand.
4   They weren't in London.

b 🔊 Play the recording, pausing after each question and answer for students to repeat. Make sure students are using the correct intonation of the questions and answers and drill these in isolation if necessary.

TAPESCRIPT
Was he only 40?
Yes, he was.
Were they in London?
No, they weren't.

c Divide the class into pairs. Ask a stronger pair to demonstrate the example dialogue. Students now continue asking and answering the questions from Exercise 2c. Monitor and check students are taking turns to ask and answer and that they are using the correct intonation and verb forms. Make a note of any repeated errors to go through as a class at the end of the exercise. Ask a few pairs to feedback to the rest of the class.

Answers
1   No, they weren't. They were in New York.
2   No, they weren't. They were on their way to a recording studio.
3   Yes, he was.
4   No, they weren't. They were in front of their apartment building.
5   Yes, he was.
6   No, there wasn't. There was a gun in his hand.
7   No, he wasn't. He was 40 years old.

4 Vocabulary and speaking

Time expressions

a Students read through the words in the box and the table. Go through the examples in the box and then give students a few minutes to complete the exercise. Check answers. Ask students to give you some examples of their own for the time expressions. Remind them that they are all past time expressions and that they should use *was/wasn't*, *were/weren't* in their examples.

Answers
Last: month, weekend
Yesterday: evening, afternoon

(b) / (c)

Divide the class into pairs. Ask a stronger pair to demonstrate the example dialogue, drawing students' attention to the use of the time from the box and a time expression from Exercise 4a. Students ask and answer. Monitor and check students are taking turns to ask and answer and that they are using the times and time expressions correctly. Make a note of any repeated errors to go through as a class after the exercise. Ask a few pairs to tell the rest of the class what they found out about their partner.

5 Listen

(a) Students read the questions and then in pairs or small groups discuss the answers and any other information they know. Elicit their responses but do not correct them at this stage.

(b) 🔊 Play the recording while students listen and check their answers. Play it a second time, pausing as necessary to clarify any problems.

TAPESCRIPT

Woman Oh, I love that song.

Boy I think I know it. Is it John Lennon?

Woman That's right. He was my favourite. I remember the day he was shot – I was really sad.

Boy When was that, Mum?

Woman 1980. December 1980. He wasn't very old – he was only 40.

Boy What was the name of that band he was in? Before he was shot?

Woman Oh, Tom – the Beatles!

Boy Oh yes, right. Of course. Were they from London?

Woman No they weren't! They were from Liverpool. Oh, they were fantastic, just wonderful.

Boy How many of them were there – in the Beatles, I mean?

Woman There were four of them – John, Paul, George and Ringo. Very young – John was my favourite.

Boy Are their songs still on the radio?

Woman Yes, they are. That song *Yesterday*, for example – that's a really famous Beatles song, they play that on the radio a lot.

Boy Oh yeah, I know that one. There was a really good song called *Miss You* on the radio last week – I think that was the Beatles too.

Woman No, Tom, I don't think so. *Miss You* was the Rolling Stones, not the Beatles.

Boy OK, if you say so, Mum. Anyway, when did the Beatles break up – when did they stop?

Woman 1970. John Lennon just said "I want to stop", and they broke up. Then they ...

Answers
1 Liverpool
2 Four
3 John, Paul, George and Ringo

(c) 🔊 Students read the questions. Elicit their responses, then play the recording again while students listen and check their answers.

Answers
1 True
2 False. Some Beatles songs are on the radio a lot.
3 False. *Miss You* was a Rolling Stones song.
4 False. They stopped in 1970.

6 Vocabulary
Ordinal number and dates

(a) Students read the sentence.

Stronger classes: They can complete the sentence and then look back at the text to check.

Weaker classes: They can read the text again before completing the sentence.

Check answers.

Answer
8 December

Look box
It may be useful to draw students' attention to the information in this box at this point. Students should be aware that dates in English are written differently from the way they are said.

(b) 🔊 Students quickly read the list of numbers. Explain that this list of numbers is written the way dates are said (refer students to the Look box if necessary). Play the recording, pausing after each number for students to repeat.

TAPESCRIPT

1st (first)   2nd (second)   3rd (third)   4th (fourth)
5th (fifth)   6th (sixth)   7th (seventh)   8th (eighth)
9th (ninth)   10th (tenth)   12th (twelfth)
13th (thirteenth)   20th (twentieth)   30th (thirtieth)

┌─ OPTIONAL ACTIVITY ══════════
Ask a student to tell the rest of the class today's date and then ask some others to give a few other significant dates of festivals or things they celebrate to make sure they have all understood.

(c) 🔊 Play the recording, pausing after the first item and go through this as an example. Play the rest of the recording while students listen and write down the numbers they hear. Students can compare answers in pairs before a whole class check. Play the recording again if necessary to clarify any problems.

third seventh tenth eleventh nineteenth twentieth twenty-third thirtieth

(d) Divide the class in pairs or if students checked answers in pairs for Exercise 6c they can stay in those pairs. Ask a stronger pair to demonstrate the example question and answer. Students then continue asking and answering about the other months. Monitor and check students are taking turns to ask and answer and that they are using ordinal numbers correctly. Make a note of any repeated errors to go through as a class after the exercise.

(e) 🔊 Students read through items 1 to 4. Play the recording, pausing after the first item and go through this as an example. Play the recording while students listen and complete the exercise. Check answers, playing and pausing the recording as necessary to clarify any problems.

TAPESCRIPT

1
Boy   When's your birthday, Jane?
Girl   The sixth of December.
Boy   The sixth of December?
Girl   Yes, that's right.

2
Girl   When's Emma's birthday?
Boy   Oh, erm … let me think. Erm … oh, yes.
      The thirteenth of June.
Girl   The thirteenth of June? Really? That's the
      same day as my grandmother's.

3
Boy   Is there a concert in January?
Girl   Yeah. It's on the fourth.
Boy   Great. Erm … let me write it down. Fourth
      of January.

4
Girl   Bye, Peter. Have a good holiday in Paris.
Boy   Oh, thanks.
Girl   When are you coming back?
Boy   Oh, … twenty-third of April.

Answers
1 b   2 a   3 a   4 b

(f) Divide the class into pairs. Students read through questions 1 to 4. Ask a stronger pair to demonstrate the question and answer for item 1. Draw students' attention to the use of ordinal numbers and dates and months in the answer. Students complete the exercise. Ask a few pairs to feedback on the information they found out about their partner.

(g) Students read through dates 1 to 5. Go through the example as a class, making sure students are clear about the differences between the written and spoken forms. Students can complete this exercise in pairs or you can ask individual students to give you the dates.

Vocabulary notebook
Encourage students to start a section called *Ordinal numbers and dates* and to note down some examples of their own.

┌ OPTIONAL ACTIVITY ─────────────────
│ Call out a number and students must give you the
│ relevant ordinal number.
└

Rob's wallet

7 Read and listen

(a) 🔊 Students read the question and predict the answer. Play the recording while students listen and read and check their predictions. How many were correct?

TAPESCRIPT
See the photo story on page 96 of the Student's Book.

Answer
His wallet isn't in his jacket pocket.

(b) Students read through sentences 1 to 5. Go through the example as a class, making sure students understand that there is something wrong with every sentence. Draw their attention to the use of the negative short answer in the first part of the answer.

Weaker classes: They can work on this in pairs.

Students complete the exercise. Check answers.

Answers
2 No, he wasn't. He was in the CD shop, the bookshop and the sports shop.
3 No, he wasn't. He was in the sports shop to buy trainers.
4 No, it wasn't. It was in the bag with his trainers.

8 Everyday English

(a) Divide the class into pairs. Students read through expressions 1 to 4. Go through the first one as a class, asking students how this would be said in L1. Students then decide how the other expressions would be said. Ask pairs to feedback to the class. Does everyone agree?

(b) Students read through dialogues 1 to 4. Check any problems. Go through the first dialogue as an example, if necessary. Students complete the exercise. They can compare answers in pairs before a whole class check.

Answers
1   You must be joking
2   Calm down
3   Oh, brilliant
4   Can I have a look

Vocabulary notebook
Encourage students to note down the Everyday English expressions and the translations.

Stronger classes: They can write their own dialogues using the expressions in Exercise 8a and then act them out.

Weaker classes: In pairs, they can act out the dialogues in Exercise 8b.

9 **Write**

Warm up

Ask students where they were on holiday last month/summer/year. Elicit some answers and then ask them if it was a good holiday.

a Students read the questions and then skim the email to find the answers. Check answers as a class.

Answers
1 In Spain.
2 Yes, it was.

b This exercise can be set for homework. Students read through the prompt questions.

Stronger classes: They can work out the questions and answer them and draft their emails. Remind them to refer to the model email in Exercise 9a if necessary. They can then write out their final versions.

Weaker classes: Go through each question as a class. Give students time to answer each question and then refer them back to the model email in Exercise 9a. Students can then decide which answers will go in which paragraph and then draft their messages. They can then check their drafts with you or a partner before they write a final version.

(14) She didn't listen

Unit overview

TOPIC: Famous people from the past

TEXTS
Reading and listening: to a text about Florence Nightingale
Listening: to a radio quiz about past events
Reading: Culture in mind: *Steve Biko*
Writing: a paragraph about a famous person for a school magazine

SPEAKING
Completing a questionnaire about past activities

LANGUAGE
Grammar: Past simple: regular verbs, statements, questions and negatives
Pronunciation: *—ed* endings
Vocabulary: Verb and noun pairs

1 Read and listen

If you set the background information as a homework research task, ask students to tell the rest of the class what they found out.

BACKGROUND INFORMATION

The Crimean War: Took place between 1853 and 1856 between Russia and Turkey, Britain, France and Sardinia. The fighting centred around Sebastopol, the main base for the Russian fleet. The city eventually fell in 1855 and the war ended.

Florence Nightingale: Was born in Florence, Italy on 12th May 1820 and died on 13th August 1910. She is said to be the founder of modern nursing and made her name during the Crimean War. In 1860 she established a nursing school at St Thomas's Hospital in London. She was the first British woman to be awarded the British Order of Merit in 1907.

Scutari: This is the old barracks hospital where Florence Nightingale was based during the Crimean War. Scutari is the Greek name for the district of Istanbul which is now known as Üsküdar. It is located on the Asian shore of the Bosphorous opposite the peninsula of Stamboul where you can find tourist sights such as the Blue Mosque, Saint Sophia and Topkapi.

Warm up

Ask students if they have ever been in hospital? If so, how was their experience? If not, have they ever visited someone? What was it like?

(a) Students read the questions.
Stronger classes: They can skim the text and find the answers.
Weaker classes: Read the text aloud as a class and then students find the answers.
Check answers.

Answers
1 It was in 1854.
2 She was born on 12 May, 1820.

(b) 🔊 Students read questions 1 to 4. Check any problems. Go through the first item as a class, if necessary. Play the recording while students complete the exercise. Students can compare answers in pairs before a whole class check. Play the recording again if necessary, pausing to clarify any problems.

TAPESCRIPT
See reading text on page 98 of the Student's Book.

Answers
1 Because there were no beds or toilets and there was blood everywhere.
2 No, they weren't.
3 After six months the hospital was clean, there were toilets and clean clothes and there was food for the soldiers.
4 Because she carried a lamp with her.

OPTIONAL ACTIVITY
Give students the following True/False activity if they need further practice.
1 The Crimean War was between Britain and France.
2 Florence Nightingale wanted to be a doctor.
3 She travelled to Scutari in 1854.
4 Florence worked with other nurses.
5 She was 90 when she died.

Answers
1 False. It was between Turkey, France, Britain and Russia.
2 False. She wanted to be a nurse.
3 True
4 True
5 True

2 Grammar

Past simple

(a) **Stronger classes:** Students read through the example sentences. Ask them what they notice about the past simple form in each sentence and elicit that *want* adds –*ed*, *study* changes the –*y* to –*i* and adds –*ed* and *travel* adds –*led*. Students can then complete the rule. Ask a few students to give you some examples of their own for these or different verbs in the past simple.

Weaker classes: Books closed. Write the following examples (or some of your own) on the board: *My brother watched TV last night. I studied Russian at school. My friend travelled to Spain by boat last summer.*

Ask students to identify the past simple form in each and elicit the rules for each verb (see Stronger classes procedure above). Students then open their books at page 99 and read the examples and complete the rule. Then ask students to give you some examples of their own.

Answer
1 –ed   2 i

> **Language note**
> Remind students that in English the past simple has the same form for all persons.

(b) Students read through the sentence parts. Go through the first item as an example, if necessary. Students complete the exercise. Check answers.

Answers
Florence Nightingale studied History and Science; visited many hospitals in Europe; died in 1910.
The soldiers called her the lady with the lamp; loved Florence Nightingale.

Regular verbs

(c) Students read the gapped text quickly. Check any problems. Go through the example as a class.

Stronger classes: They can complete the exercise on their own.

Weaker classes: Elicit the past simple form of the verbs in the box and put them on the board. Students then use those forms to complete the text.

Do not check answers at this stage.

Answers
1 died   2 liked   3 liked   4 wanted   5 started
6 listened   7 studied   8 asked

Grammar notebook
Encourage students to note down the rules for the past simple and some examples of their own for each ending.

┌─ OPTIONAL ACTIVITY ────────────
Call out some regular base forms of your own and ask students to give you the regular past simple form and then spell it out.

3 Pronunciation

–*ed* endings

(a) ◁⟩) Students read through the sentences. Play the recording, pausing after each sentence for students to repeat. Make sure students are pronouncing each ending clearly and play the recording again if there are any problems.

Stronger classes: You can ask students to read out the sentences with the correct pronunciation before listening. They can then listen and check.

TAPESCRIPT
1   We watched a film.
2   I called a friend.
3   He wanted an ice cream.

(b) ◁⟩) Play the recording, pausing after each verb for students to repeat.

TAPESCRIPT
phoned   visited   lived   walked   asked   started

(c) **Weaker classes:** Play the recording again, pausing after the first item and go through this as an example, showing students which column it should go in. Play the rest of the recording while students listen. Students complete the exercise.

Stronger classes: Students can complete the table in Exercise 3c and can listen and check only.

TAPESCRIPT
See tapescript for Exercise 3b.

Answers
/t/: walked, asked
/d/: phoned, lived
/id/: visited, started

┌─ OPTIONAL ACTIVITY ────────────
Students can go through the verbs in Exercise 2c and decide which column they would go in.

Answers
/t/: liked
/d/: watched, asked, died, listened, studied
/ɪd/: wanted, started

4 Listen

(a) Divide the class into pairs. Students read through questions 1 to 5 and answers a to e. Go through the first question and answer as an example, if necessary.

Students work in their pairs to ask and answer the questions. Monitor and check students are taking turns to ask and answer and that they are using the dates correctly. Make a note of any repeated errors to go through as a class after the exercise. Do not give answers at this stage.

b 🔊 Play the recording while students listen and check their answers to Exercise 4a.

TAPESCRIPT

Host Hello, and welcome back, and in the next round of our quiz we are looking at important dates, OK?

Woman Yes, OK.

Host And here is the first question: U.S. President J.F. Kennedy died on 22 November. In which year?

Woman Er ... I think it was in 1963.

Host And 22 November 1963 is ... absolutely correct. Kennedy died on November 22nd 1963. He was shot in Dallas, Texas. That's 20 points for you. And here's our next question. When did the first man land on the moon? Was it
a. on July 20 1949? b. on July 20 1959?
or c. on July 20 1969?

Woman Oh ... er ... the man's name was Neil Armstrong. And I think it was 1959, so ... 'b'.

Host Well, Sarah, you're right about Neil Armstrong – but he didn't land on the moon in 1959, it was on July 20th 1969. So no points for that, I'm afraid. Let's look at the next question. You can get 40 points this time. The question is about the Olympic Games in Sydney, Australia. They started on September 15th and ended on October 1st. In which year?
a. 1999? b. 2000? c. 2001?

Woman In 2000.

Host That's absolutely correct. 40 points for you. The Sydney Olympic Games started on September 15th and they ended on October 1st 2000.

And now Sarah – 100 points on the all or nothing question. In which year was Florence Nightingale born?

Woman Erm ... Oh, I'm not sure!! Er ... was it .... 1850?

Host Oh, I'm sorry, Sarah. It was in 1820, not 1850. Sorry about that, but you get a wonderful prize ...

Answers
1 c 2 a 3 e 4 b 5 d

┌─ **OPTIONAL ACTIVITY** ─────────

Stronger classes: Students can write their own past simple quiz questions and work with a partner who must answer them correctly.

Weaker classes: Elicit some key dates and events in the students' own countries or in the world and students then use these to write their own quiz questions to ask a partner.

5 Grammar
Past simple: questions and negatives

a Students read through the words in the box and questions 1 to 3. Go through the first question as an example, if necessary. Give students a few minutes to complete the gaps.

Answers
1 did, die 2 did, land 3 didn't land

b Students read the examples. Elicit the negative (*didn't die*) and question forms (*did ... go / did ... end*) and ask students how each is formed (negative uses *did + not*, questions use *did +* base form). Students then read and complete the rule before completing the table. Check answers as a class.

Answers
Rule: didn't; did
Table
Question: Did
Short answer: didn't

> **Language note**
> Students may produce question forms like ~~Did she liked the film?~~ Remind them that in questions we use *did +* base form. Remind students that we do not repeat the main verb in short answers in English.

c This exercise can be set for homework. Students read through sentences 1 to 5. Go through the example as a class, if necessary. Draw students' attention to the fact they have to think of appropriate endings for the last three items. Students complete the exercise. Check answers, making sure students are using the negative form correctly.

Answers
2 didn't use
3 didn't watch (the news)
4 didn't travel (to Paris)
5 didn't visit (their teachers)

d This exercise can be set for homework. Students read through sentences 1 to 5. Go through the example as a class, if necessary. Students complete the exercise. Check answers, making sure students are using the question form correctly.

Answers
2 did it happen
3 did they study
4 did you have a pizza
5 did you go

Grammar notebook

Remind students to make a note of the rules and to write some examples of their own for past simple questions and negatives.

⌐ OPTIONAL ACTIVITY ━━━━━━━━━━

What did I do last night?

This can be done as a whole class activity or in small groups. One student thinks of something they did at the weekend or last night. The others must guess using past simple verbs (within a time limit) what the person was doing. The person replying must use short answers. The student who guesses the action correctly takes the next turn. For example:

S2: Did you watch TV?
S1: No, I didn't.
S3: Did you do your homework?
S1: No, I didn't.
S4: Did you read a book?
S1: Yes, I did.

6 Speak

(a) Students read the questionnaire. Check any problems. Go through the first item as an example, if necessary. Give students a few minutes to complete their answers.

(b) Divide the class into pairs. Ask a stronger pair to demonstrate the example question and answer. Draw students' attention to the use of the past simple question and the short answer. Students ask and answer to complete the *My partner* column in the questionnaire in Exercise 6a. Monitor and check students are taking turns to ask and answer and that they are using the question and short answer forms correctly. Ask pairs to feedback to the class on what they found out about their partner.

(c) Students work with a new partner. Ask a stronger pair to demonstrate the example question and answer. Draw students' attention to the use of the *Wh–* questions with the past simple and the past simple positive form in the answers. Give students a few minutes to exchange information. Monitor and check students are taking turns to ask and answer and that they are using the question and short answer forms correctly. Ask pairs to feedback to the class on what they found out about their partner.

7 Vocabulary

Verb and noun pairs

(a) **Stronger classes:** Students read through the nouns in the box and look at the table headings. Go through the example as a class. Students complete the exercise. Check answers.

Weaker classes: Write the verbs from the table on the board and elicit any nouns which go with them which students already know. If they don't know any already

then give them an example of your own for each heading. Students then open their books at page 101 and read through the nouns in the box. Ask for volunteers to come out and write each noun under the appropriate heading. The rest of the class can decide if each noun is placed under the correct heading.

Answers
have: a coffee, (an) ice cream
practise: English
play: sports
go to: bed, school, the cinema

(b) Students read through the list of nouns and classify them under the correct heading in the table in Exercise 7a. Check answers as a class.

Answers
have: breakfast/lunch/dinner, a party, a bath
practise: the piano
play: the piano
go to: work, a party

Vocabulary notebook

Encourage students to start a section called *Verb and noun pairs*. They can then copy down the completed table from Exercises 7a and b or they can start a section for each verb and add nouns to it as they come across them.

⌐ OPTIONAL ACTIVITY ━━━━━━━━━━━━━━━━━━━

Can students add any more nouns to the verbs in Exercise 7?

Culture in mind

8 Read

If you set the background information as a homework research task, ask students to tell the rest of the class what they found out.

BACKGROUND INFORMATION

Steve Biko: Was born in 1946 in King Williams Town, Cape Province and died in 1977. He was a famous South African political activist who was the leader of the Black Consciousness Movement. He studied at Natal University where he became involved in politics. He was one of the founders and the first president of the all-black South African student organisation in 1969. He died in police custody. A film was made about his life in 1987 by Sir Richard Attenborough called *Cry Freedom*.

South Africa: Is officially called the Republic of South Africa. It is situated in the southern part of the continent of Africa and has borders with the Atlantic Ocean in the west, Namibia in the north west, Botswana and Zimbabwe in the north, Mozambique and Swaziland in the north east and the Indian Ocean in the south and east. Three of its main cities are Pretoria (the administrative capital), Cape Town (the legislative capital) and Bloemfontein (the judicial capital).

Port Elizabeth: Is a city in the Cape province of South Africa. It is located on the southern coast. It is mainly an industrial city and was founded in 1820 by British settlers.

Nelson Mandela: Was born Nelson Rolihlahla Mandela on July 18th 1918 in Transkei, South Africa. His father was a Xhosa chief and Mandela studied law and set up a practice in Johannesburg in 1952. He was a resistance leader who opposed apartheid and he spent 27 years in prison, many of them on Robben Island. He was freed from Verster Prison on February 11th 1990 and on April 27th 1994 the first free elections were held in South Africa. The African National Congress won over 62% of the votes and Nelson Mandela was the first president of a black-ruled South Africa. He was awarded the Nobel Peace Prize.

Warm up

Books closed. Give students a world map (or use a map in the class) and ask them to locate South Africa. Ask them if they know what European languages are spoken in South Africa (English and Afrikaans). Pre-teach any vocabulary, e.g. *vote*, *against*, *government*, *prison*, *beat*, *become*.

a) Students open their books at page 102 and read the questions. Elicit their responses.

Stronger classes: They can skim the text and check their answers.

Weaker classes: Read the text aloud as a class and then ask students to check their answers.

Answers
1 Students' own answers
2 Apartheid was the separation of black and white people.

b) Students read through statements 1 to 7. You may want to pre-teach the irregular verbs *could* and *went*. Go through the first item as an example, if necessary. Students read the text again and complete the exercise. Check answers. Encourage them to correct the false answers.

Answers
1 True
2 False. Many white South Africans hated this system.
3 True
4 True
5 False. He went to prison again in 1977.
6 False. It ended in 1991.

7 False. Nelson Mandela was the first black president.

c) In pairs or small groups, students discuss the question and then feedback to the rest of the class.

9 Write

a) Ask students when Lady Diana Spencer died. Students read the text quickly and find the answer.

Answer
She died on 31 August 1997.

b) This exercise can be done in pairs and can be set for homework. Students decide on a famous person they would like to write about. It can be someone from their own country or someone from somewhere else.

Stronger classes: They must then decide on the key facts they want to include in their article about that person's life.

Weaker classes: Refer students back to the Steve Biko text on page 102 and the Diana Spencer text. Encourage them to look at the text structure and decide on the sort of information they want to include in each paragraph.

Students can draft their articles and then check them with another pair/student. They can then write a final version.

Encourage students to add pictures or illustrations to their texts.

OPTIONAL ACTIVITY
Students can vote for the best texts and these could be displayed on the classroom wall or if there is a school magazine students could submit their articles for publication.

15 Where did they go?

Unit overview

TOPIC: Past mysteries

TEXTS

Reading and listening: to a text about the disappearance of Lord Lucan
Listening: to a radio interview about Lord Lucan
Reading: a text about the mystery of the *Mary Celeste*
Reading and listening: photo story: *Who's Caroline?*
Writing: a story about a strange place

SPEAKING

Retelling a story from pictures
Making guesses about past and present situations

LANGUAGE

Grammar: Past simple: irregular verbs
Vocabulary: Adverbs; Everyday English: *Like my new coat?*; *No idea.*
Pronunciation: Adverbs

1 Read and listen

a Students read through items 1 to 3 and look at the photo. Elicit their responses. Do not give answers at this point.

b Students read the text quickly and check their answer to Exercise 1a (a man who disappeared).

Weaker classes: You may want to pre-teach the following vocabulary: *good-looking, gambling, casino, live apart.*

c 🔊 Students read through questions 1 to 4. Check any problems. Go through the first item as an example, if necessary.

Stronger classes: They can answer the questions and then can listen and read to check.

Weaker classes: Play the recording while students listen and read only. Students complete the exercise.

Check answers, playing and pausing the recording again as necessary to clarify any problems.

TAPESCRIPT

See reading text on page 104 of the Student's Book.

Answers

1 He liked gambling on horse races.
2 He started to lose a lot of money and he lived apart from his wife.
3 No one knows where he went.
4 No one knows where he is now.

2 Listen

a 🔊 Give students a few minutes to look at the pictures.

Stronger classes: Students can try to predict the order of the pictures and can then listen and check their predictions.

Weaker classes: After students have looked at the pictures, elicit what they think is happening in each and write the prompts on the board. Play the recording while students listen only. Students then work out the order of the pictures. Students can compare answers in pairs.

Play the recording again, pausing after each picture for students to see the correct order.

TAPESCRIPT

Man   Today we're talking to Professor Jean Smithson, about the Lord Lucan mystery. Professor Smithson, good morning. Can you tell us about Lord Lucan? What happened to him?

Woman   Good morning. Well, we don't know what happened to him. But we do know some things – for example, we know about his wife and we know about Sandra Rivett.

Man   Sandra Rivett? Who was she?

Woman   She was the young woman who looked after Lord Lucan's children. And on November 7 1974, somebody killed her in a room in Lord Lucan's house.

Man   Lord Lucan himself? Did he kill her?

Woman   Well, we don't know for sure, but many people think he did. But we do know that Lord Lucan's wife, Lady Lucan, was in the house that day. She heard a noise and went downstairs. She opened the door, and saw Sandra dead. Then somebody tried to kill her too, and ran away. But Lady Lucan wasn't dead. The police think that Lord Lucan wanted to kill his wife, and killed Sandra Rivett by mistake.

Man   But they don't know for sure?

Woman   No. The police went to the house, and of course Lord Lucan wasn't there. But, the police found a note that he left. In the note, Lord Lucan said that he didn't kill the woman.

Man   Did they find anything else?

Woman   Well, they found out that Lord Lucan went to a friend's house and took a car. He drove the car out of London. He went down to the south of England, near the sea, and he left the car there. And he – disappeared!

Man   Nobody saw him again.

Woman   That's right. The police found Lord Lucan's passport and his money.

Man So he didn't leave England.

Woman Well, perhaps he did. It's possible to leave with no passport if you are rich and have the right friends! But we still don't really know. He is probably dead, but no one found his body, so we can't be 100% sure.

Man A terrible story. Thank you, Professor Smithson. OK, let's ...

Answers

a 3   b 4   c 5   e 6   f 2

(b) In pairs or small groups, students discuss the question and then feedback to the rest of the class.

3 Grammar
Past simple: irregular verbs

(a) **Stronger classes:** Students read the examples. Explain that these are irregular past simple forms, and elicit a few regular past simple forms so that students can see the difference. Students then go back through the article on page 104 and underline other past simple irregulars. Check answers.

Students then read through the verbs in the table. Go through the example as a class. Students then use the Irregular verb list on page 122 to help them complete it. Alternatively, if you feel students are capable enough, ask them to predict the past simple forms for each verb and then use the Irregular verb list to check their predictions.

They can compare answers in pairs before a whole class check.

Weaker classes: Books closed. Elicit a few regular past simple forms and write them on the board. Then write the following base forms (or ones of your own choice) on the board: *have*, *know*, *go*. Ask students if they can guess what the past simple forms of these verbs are. Explain that they are irregular so will not follow the pattern for regular verbs. Elicit or give the past simple forms of the base forms. Students then open their books at page 105 and read the examples. Follow the procedure for Stronger classes from this point.

Answers

find – found
get – got
go – went
run – ran
say – said
see – saw
speak – spoke
take – took
tell – told
think – thought
wake – woke

Language note

It may be helpful for students to know the other past simple irregular forms:

Negative: *did not / didn't* + base form, e.g. *didn't tell* NOT ~~*didn't told*~~

Question: *did* + subject + base form, e.g. *Did she tell ...?* NOT ~~*Did she told ...?*~~

Short answers: Do not repeat the main verb, e.g. *Yes, she did. / No, she didn't.*

OPTIONAL ACTIVITY

Stronger classes: Students can make sentences of their own using the past simple forms of the verbs in Exercise 3a.

Weaker classes: You can call out a base form from Exercise 3a and ask students to supply the past simple form.

(b) Students read through sentences 1 to 4. Go through the example as a class, drawing students' attention to the past simple positive form. Students complete the exercise. Remind them that they may need to use all the different forms of the past simple in the exercise. Check answers.

Answers

1 Did; write
2 Did, see; saw
3 Did, go; went
4 Did, get; got

(c) Students read through the gapped text. Check any problems.

Stronger classes: They can complete the text with the past simple form of the verbs in the box.

Weaker classes: Elicit or give the past simple form of the verbs in the box and write them on the board. Go through the example as a class. Students complete the exercise.

Check answers as a class.

Answers

1 wrote   2 became   3 had   4 knew   5 went
6 spoke

Grammar notebook

Encourage students to start a section called *Past simple: irregular verbs*. Remind them to make a note of the past simple from this exercise and to write down translations if necessary.

OPTIONAL ACTIVITY

Whole class. Past simple bingo. Students write down e.g. six verbs of their own choice in the base form. You then call out irregular past simple forms (keeping a note of the verbs you have called out). The student who crosses off all their base forms first and shouts Bingo! is the winner. Check the verbs they wrote down and the verbs you called out to make sure they have marked off the correct ones.

4 Speak

(a) Divide the class into pairs.

Stronger classes: Students look at the pictures and decide on the correct order.

Weaker classes: Go through each picture as a class, eliciting what is happening. Students then work out the order of events using this information.

Check answers as a class.

Answers
a 4
b 3
c 2
d 6
e 1
f 5

(b) In pairs students now tell the story using the past simple. Ask a stronger pair to give you the past simple sentence for the first picture. Students continue like this in their pairs. Monitor and check students are taking turns to say the sentences. Make sure they are using the past simple forms correctly and make a note of any repeated errors to go through as a class after the exercise. Ask a few pairs to read out their sentences to the rest of the class.

Suggested answers
1 He woke up late.
2 He had a shower.
3 He got dressed.
4 He ran to school.
5 He arrived at school. No one was there!
6 He got back home. He saw the clock. It was five past seven.

─ OPTIONAL ACTIVITY ─────────
Ask students if they have ever had an experience similar to the boy in Exercise 4. If so, ask them to tell the rest of the class what happened using the past simple.

5 Read

If you set the background information as a homework research task, ask students to tell the rest of the class what they found out.

BACKGROUND INFORMATION
Mary Celeste: The ship left New York in early November 1872. She had 1709 barrels of grain alcohol on board bound for Genoa in Italy. The ship and her cargo never arrived at their destination.

Warm up

Ask students if they have heard of the ship the *Mary Celeste* and elicit what they know about it.

(a) Students read through questions 1 to 4. Check any problems. Students read the text and answer the questions. Go through the first item as an example, if necessary.

Weaker classes: You may want to pre-teach the following vocabulary: *out of control, signals, crew, noisy, busy, nowhere, danger, iceberg, storm, monster.* Check answers as a class.

Answers
1 They went on board on December 5 1872.
2 Because there was no one on the ship.
3 There were ten people on board: seven crew members, Captain Briggs, his wife and daughter.
4 Because there were cups of tea and food on the tables.

(b) In pairs or small groups, students discuss the question. Ask pairs/groups to feedback to the rest of the class.

6 Vocabulary
Adverbs

(a) **Stronger classes:** Students read through the examples from the listening text. Draw their attention to the adverbs in each sentence and ask them which adjectives each adverb comes from (sudden/quick). Elicit how an adverb is formed (add –*ly* to the adjective). Students then read and complete the rule.

Weaker classes: Books closed. Write the following adjectives on the board (or some of your own choice): *quiet, quick, sudden.* Explain that they are going to change those adjectives into adverbs, making sure they understand what an adverb is. Ask them to think about how an adverb is formed and elicit or give them the rule: add –*ly* to the adjective. Students open their books at page 107 and read the examples. They can then complete the rule.

Answer
–*ly*

─ OPTIONAL ACTIVITY ─────────
Call out a few more adjectives of your own choice and ask students to supply you with the adverbs.

(b) Students read through adjectives in the box. Go through the example as a class.

Stronger classes: They can make the adjectives into adverbs and then put them into sentences 1 to 7.

Weaker classes: Go through each adjective as a class, eliciting the correct adverb. Students then read through sentences 1 to 7. Check any problems and go through the example as a class. Students complete the exercise. Check answers.

Answers
Adjectives: angrily, slowly, quickly, suddenly, carefully, badly
Sentences: 2 slowly   3 quickly   4 carefully
5 badly   6 suddenly   7 angrily

Grammar notebook

Remind students to start a section called *Adverbs* and to note down the adverbs from this exercise and any translations which will help them.

7 Pronunciation

Adverbs

🔊 Students read through adverbs 1 to 7 quickly. Play the recording, pausing after each word for students to repeat.

TAPESCRIPT

1 quietly   2 suddenly   3 probably   4 quickly
5 carefully   6 slowly   7 angrily

┌─ OPTIONAL ACTIVITY ─────────
│ Whole class or small groups. Students can choose
│ an adverb from Exercises 6 and 7 and mime doing an
│ action in that way. The rest of the class/group must
│ guess the action and the adverb correctly before they
│ can have a turn.

8 Speak

a Students read through the questions and the examples. Elicit the answers.

Answers
1 We use *maybe* and *perhaps* if we are unsure something has happened.
2 We use *probably* when we are more certain that something has happened and there is evidence to suggest an event took place.

b Divide the class into pairs. Refer students back to the conversations they had in Exercise 5b about what they thought happened to the *Mary Celeste*. Ask a stronger pair to demonstrate the example dialogue.

Stronger classes: They can come up with new theories about the *Mary Celeste* using the language in Exercise 8a.

Weaker classes: Elicit their ideas from Exercise 5b or elicit some new ones and encourage them to express their ideas using the language from Exercise 8a.

Ask pairs to feedback to the rest of the class.

c Divide the class into pairs or students can work in the same pairs as they did in Exercise 8b. Give students a few minutes to look at the pictures. Elicit what they think the things might be. Ask a stronger pair to demonstrate the example dialogue, drawing students' attention to the use of *perhaps* and *maybe*. Give students time to ask and answer about each picture. Monitor and check students are taking turns to do this before asking pairs to feedback to the class.

Who's Caroline?

9 Read and listen

a 🔊 Students read the title and the questions. Elicit their predictions. Play the recording while students read and listen and check their predictions. How many were correct?

TAPESCRIPT
See the photo story on page 108 of the Student's Book.

Answer
Alex bought a coat with a hole in the pocket and found a photo of a girl in the pocket. He went back to the shop and gave the photo to another boy called Alex.

b Students read through the gapped text. Check any problems. Go through the example as a class, drawing students' attention to the past simple. Students complete the exercise. Remind them they will need to use regular and irregular past simple forms. Remind them to check the irregular verb list if they need help with any irregular past simple forms. Check answers.

Answers
1 went   2 showed   3 found   4 thought   5 had
6 went   7 was   8 asked   9 gave   10 said
11 was

┌─ OPTIONAL ACTIVITY ─────────
│ In groups of four students can act out the dialogue
│ from Exercise 9.

10 Everyday English

a **Stronger classes:** They can read the expressions and decide who says them without looking back. They can look back to check their answers.

Weaker classes: Students read the two expressions and then locate them in the photo story on page 108 and decide who said them.

Answers
1 Alex   2 Alex

Go through the rest of the information as a class.

b Divide the class into pairs. Students discuss what the full questions are for the expressions in Exercise 10a. Ask pairs to feedback to the rest of the class. Does everyone agree?

Answers
1 Do you like my new coat?
2 I've no idea.

c Students read dialogues 1 and 2. Check any problems. Then in pairs they discuss what the full questions are. Ask pairs to feedback to the rest of the class.

Answers
1 Are you hungry?; Do you want to have lunch?
2 Have you got a minute?; Do you want me to help you?

11 Write

a Students read through questions 1 to 4. Check any
problems. Students then read the letter quickly and
answer the questions. Check answers.

Answers
1   He visited a castle.
2   It was very dark and cold.
3   A man with very long arms and legs.
4   The guide disappeared when Josh went into
    the shop.

b This exercise can be set for homework. Students read
through the words in the box. Check any problems.

Stronger classes: Students can use Josh's letter and
the words in the box, adding more of their own, to
write a letter. Remind them to plan the letter first
before drafting and then producing a final version.

Weaker classes: Students can work on this in pairs.
Elicit a few more words to help students with their
letters if necessary. Encourage them to plan and draft
their letter before producing a final version. Once
drafts have been checked students can write a final
version.

16 Now and then

Unit overview

TOPIC: Comparing life in the past with life now

TEXTS
Listening: to a dialogue comparing life now and in the past
Reading: a text about an island chef in Los Angeles
Reading: Culture in mind: *UK holiday camps*
Writing: a competition entry

SPEAKING
Describing things
Comparing people, places and objects

LANGUAGE
Grammar: Comparison of adjectives
Pronunciation: *than* /ðən/
Vocabulary: adjectives and opposites

1 Listen

If you set the background information as a homework research task, ask students to tell the rest of the class what they found out.

BACKGROUND INFORMATION

Piccadilly Circus: Is an area of central London near Trafalgar Square. It has lots of neon signs and advertisements and the statue of Eros is the central point. It is a common meeting place for people in that part of London.

Warm up

Books closed. Ask students to think about how their own town/city may have changed over the years. Elicit the differences and the things that have stayed the same.

a Students open their books at page 110 and look at the photos. In pairs or small groups, students discuss the similarities and differences between the two photos. Ask pairs/groups to feedback to the rest of the class.

b 🔊 Students read through items 1 to 6. Check any problems. Play the recording, pausing after the first item is mentioned and go through this as an example. Play the rest of the recording while students listen only. Give students a few minutes to answer the questions. Check answers as a class, playing and pausing the recording again to clarify any problems.

Weaker classes: You can divide this into two parts. Students can listen to the recording for grandfather only and then mark the things he mentions. Students then listen to Lucy talking and mark the things she mentions.

TAPESCRIPT

Old man I think life was good for me when I was younger, when I was a teenager. Yes, life was good. Is it better now? No, I don't think so, not really. But it's very different! I think perhaps life is more interesting now – you know, there are computers and DVDs, and things like that. When I was young, of course, we didn't even have television! So it wasn't very exciting. But I think that life is more difficult for today's teenagers than it was for me – for example, my granddaughter Lucy. Her school work – she gets a lot of homework to do, and she has lots of tests and exams – it wasn't like that for me. I was freer than her, I think. I think school life is more difficult now, certainly. But you know, I think perhaps she's happier than I was!

Lucy I think perhaps that some things are easier now – for example, with mobile phones and email, I can talk to my friends any time I want to. But I also know that some things now are difficult for my granddad. I'm sure that now, life is faster than in the 1950s, and I think that's hard for him. I mean, now he's older, so of course things are more difficult – like, walking in the streets in the town, it's hard for him, the streets are very crowded, I think they're more crowded than before – and there are a lot more cars these days, the roads are much busier than in the 1950s. And I'm sure that things in the shops are more expensive! So perhaps life is worse for him now – but he's still a happy man!

Answers
1 L   2 G   3 G   4 L   5 G   6 L

c 🔊 **Stronger classes:** They can mark the sentences true or false and then listen again to check only.

Weaker classes: Play each recording again while students listen only. Go through the first item as an example, if necessary. Students complete the exercise.

Check answers, encouraging students to correct the false answers.

Answers
1 False. He doesn't think life is better now.
2 True
3 False. He thinks that life is more difficult for her.
4 False. It's hard for him because the streets are so crowded.
5 True

2 Grammar

Comparison of adjectives

(a) 🔊 **Stronger classes:** Students read through the sentences. Go through the first one as an example, if necessary. Students complete the exercise. Play the recording for Exercise 1b again for students to check answers.

Weaker classes: Play the recording again and then students complete the exercise. Play it a second time to check answers.

TAPESCRIPT
See tapescript for Exercise 1b above.

Answers

2 L 3 L 4 G 5 G 6 G 7 G 8 L

(b) Students read through the table. Elicit what they notice about the comparative form of older and elicit that *–er* has been added to *old*. Explain to them that the adjectives used in the sentences in Exercise 2a were used to show comparisons. Students now go back through the sentences in Exercise 2a and underline the adjectives and the words which show comparison. Go through the first item as a class, if necessary. Students then use this information to help them fill in the table.

Check answers as a class.

Answers

younger   happier   more   more   better   worse

Students use the information from the table to complete the rules in the box. Check answers.

Weaker classes: Elicit the rules as a class then students complete them.

Answers

• *i*
• more
• worse

To check understanding at this point, give students a few adjectives of your own and ask them to give you the comparative forms.

(c) Students read through adjectives 1 to 8. Check any problems. Go through the first one as an example, if necessary. Students complete the exercise. Remind them to think carefully about whether the adjective is regular, has a spelling change or is irregular. They can compare answers in pairs before a whole class check.

Answers

1 nearer   2 taller   3 cheaper   4 funnier
5 more important   6 faster   7 more expensive
8 hotter

(d) Students read through sentences 1 to 6. Go through the example as a class, drawing students' attention to the adjective and its comparative form. Students complete the exercise.

Weaker classes: Elicit the adjectives students will have to use for each sentence as a class and write them on the board. Students then complete the exercise. Check answers.

Answers

2 fast, faster
3 funny, funnier
4 near, nearer
5 expensive, more expensive
6 tall, taller

than

(e) Students read the example sentences. Ask them which other words are used with the comparative adjectives to show comparison and elicit *than*. Ask them to provide another example of their own using an adjective from Exercise 2c.

> **Language notes**
> 1 Students may produce statements like ~~Delhi is hotter that~~ ... because of the way their own language works. Remind them that in English we use *than* with comparative adjectives when comparing two things.
> 2 Remind them too that we do not say ~~I am more tall than you~~.

(f) Students now look at the sentences in Exercise 2d again and rewrite them using *than*. Go through the example as a class. Students complete the exercise. Check answers.

Answers

2 Planes are faster than trains.
3 Annie's joke was funnier than Mike's joke.
4 Moreton's nearer than Haytown.
5 The Plaza Hotel's more expensive than the Grand Hotel.
6 Andy's taller than Matt.

Grammar notebook

Remind students to copy their completed table into their notebooks and to make a note of any translations that they will find helpful.

Weaker classes: Call out an adjective and ask students to give you the comparative form.

3 Pronunciation

than /ðən/

(a) ◁))) Students read through sentences 1 to 5. Play the recording while students listen. Elicit the pronunciation of *than* after they have heard all five sentences.

TAPESCRIPT
1 She's taller than me.
2 I'm older than him.
3 It's hotter than yesterday.
4 Our dog's bigger than yours.
5 This is more expensive than that one.

(b) ◁))) Play the recording again, pausing after each sentence for students to repeat. Make sure students are pronouncing *than* correctly. If they are still having problems, drill one or two of the sentences as a class.

4 Speak

Divide the class into pairs. Ask a stronger student to demonstrate the example sentence, drawing students' attention to the use of comparatives. Students then exchange information about things and people using comparatives. Monitor and check students are taking turns to exchange information and that they are using the comparative forms correctly. Make a note of any repeated errors to go through as a class after the exercise. Ask pairs to feedback to the rest of the class on what they found out.

5 Read

If you set the background information as a homework research task, ask students to tell the rest of the class what they found out.

BACKGROUND INFORMATION

Tobermory: Is the main town on the Scottish island of Mull. It is famous for its colourfully painted houses on the waterfront.

Mull: Is an island which lies just off the west coast of Scotland.

Los Angeles: Is a US city in the state of California. It is situated on the Pacific Ocean. It is the second largest city in the USA. It is a popular tourist destination with its many parks, museums, beaches and educational institutions.

(a) Divide the class into pairs. Students look at the photos and read the questions. Give them a few minutes to discuss the questions and elicit suggestions. Students then read the article to check their answers. Were they correct?

Weaker classes: This can be done as a whole class activity and the article can be read aloud to check answers. You may want to pre-teach the following vocabulary: *chef, trip, popular, miss, earn, good luck.*

Answers
He is a chef. He lives in L.A. He is from Tobermory on the island of Mull, Scotland.

(b) Students read through questions 1 to 4. Check any problems.

Stronger classes: They can answer the questions and then can compare answers in pairs.

Weaker classes: Go through the first item as an example and then students can read the text again before answering the others.

Check answers.

Answers
1 He worked in a small café in Tobermory.
2 He misses the peace and quiet of Mull.
3 He likes Los Angeles because it is more exciting and busier than Mull and there are more things to do.
4 Perhaps when he is older. He enjoys his job in L.A. and he earns more money.

6 Vocabulary

Adjectives

(a) Students read the questions and sentences 1 to 3. Elicit the answer (sentence 3). Ask students to work out what the adjective is which each comparative adjective comes from in sentences 1 to 3.

Answers
1 modern, exciting
2 noisy, busy
3 safe, quiet

(b) Give students a few minutes to read the words in the box and look at the pictures. Check any problems. Go through the example as a class, if necessary. Students complete the exercise.

Answers
2 safe   3 noisy   4 modern   5 old-fashioned
6 boring   7 exciting   8 quiet

Language note
Remind students that in English adjectives do not agree with the subject. We don't say ~~three moderns houses~~. Remind them too that adjectives usually go before the noun they are describing, e.g. we say *a modern house* NOT ~~a house modern~~.

(c) Students read through adjectives 1 to 4. Go through the first item as an example if necessary. Students complete the exercise. They can compare answers in pairs before a whole class check.

Answers

1 boring   2 safe   3 quiet   4 old-fashioned

Vocabulary notebook

Encourage students to start a section called *Adjectives* and to note down any adjective and any translations they find helpful.

┌─ OPTIONAL ACTIVITY ─────────────

Students can make up a sentence using one or more of the adjectives in Exercise 6.

7 Speak

a Divide the class into pairs. Ask a stronger pair to demonstrate the example dialogue, drawing students' attention to the use of adjectives. Students exchange information about things in their life. Remind them to use adjectives where possible. Monitor and check students are taking turns to exchange information and that they are using the adjective in the correct position and in the correct way. Make a note of any repeated errors to go through as a class after the exercise. Ask pairs to feedback to the rest of the class.

Weaker classes: They may find it helpful if you elicit different areas of their life they can talk about and put them on the board to refer to while they are exchanging information.

b Divide the class into pairs. Students read through the topics in the box. Check any problems. Ask a stronger pair to demonstrate the example dialogue, drawing students' attention to the adjective in the first statement and the comparative in the second statement.

Stronger students: They can choose their own topics or add to the topics in the box.

Culture in mind

8 Read

Warm up

Books closed. Ask students what kinds of holidays they go on. Ask them if they have ever been to a holiday camp. If so, what kind of camp was it? Did they enjoy it? If not, ask them to imagine what a holiday camp might be like.

a Students open their books at page 114 and look at the photos and read the questions. Elicit suggestions but do not give answers at this stage.

b Students read the text and check their answers.

Weaker classes: You may want to pre-teach the following vocabulary: *escape, seaside, countryside, organised* (adj and v), *shows, loudspeaker system, luxury*.

c Students read through sentences 1 to 6. Check any problems.

Stronger classes: They can mark the sentences and then read the text again to check their answers.

Weaker classes: Students read the text again. Go through the first item as an example. Students complete the exercise.

Check answers, encouraging students to correct the false answers.

Answers

1 True
2 True
3 False. They were never quiet: loudspeakers told people when to come to breakfast and gave other messages or played music all day.
4 True
5 True
6 False. This is the temperature inside the glass building where the pools are.

9 Write

a Pre-teach the meaning of *ago*. Students then read the competition entry quickly and answer the questions.

Answers

1 You can win 500 Euros.
2 No more than 120.

b Students read Claudia's entry and decide which option she chose (A).

c This exercise can be set for homework. Students choose which option they want to write about.

Stronger classes: They can plan their text using Claudia's text as a model. Remind them to use adjectives and make comparisons where possible.

Weaker classes: Elicit some ideas with them for each of the options. Students can then draft each paragraph using Claudia's text as a model. Students swap drafts with a partner to check before preparing a final version.

┌─ OPTIONAL ACTIVITY ─────────────

Ask students to read out their entries to the rest of the class. The entries can be displayed around the classroom and students can add photos and illustrations if they wish.

Module 4 **Check your progress**

1 **Grammar**

(a) 1 were 2 was 3 was 4 Were 5 wasn't
6 were 7 were 8 weren't

(b) 1 told 2 lived 3 went 4 became 5 thought
6 left 7 died 8 found 9 learned/learnt

(c) 2 Did, go
3 Did, see
4 Did, speak
5 did, understand

(d) 2 wrote, didn't write
3 came, didn't come
4 ate, didn't eat
5 saw, didn't see

(e) 2 hotter 3 easier 4 funnier 5 happier

(f) 2 My uncle's car is more expensive than my father's.
3 Your homework is more important than that computer game.
4 Her History teacher is better than my teacher.
5 The weather in winter is worse than in summer.

2 **Vocabulary**

(a) 2 f 3 b 4 a 5 e 6 c

(b) 2 badly 3 angry 4 carefully 5 slowly 6 well
7 quickly 8 suddenly

(c) have: a look, an ice cream, a cup of tea
play: the piano, cards, football
go to: work, the cinema, bed

3 **Everyday English**

2 Calm down
3 Can I have a look
4 You must be joking
5 Oh, brilliant

How did you do?
Check that students are marking their scores. Collect these in and check them as necessary and discuss any further work needed with specific students.

Project 1

Warm up

Ask students who their favourite band is. Ask them what kind of music they sing, how many members are in the band and where they come from. Ask students if they know the band Coldplay, then give them a few minutes to read the text quickly.

Divide the class into groups of three or four.

1 Do your research

(a) **Stronger classes:** This part of the exercise can be set for homework. Each student can research the questions and then bring in the information they have collected to discuss in their group.

Weaker classes: Read through the prompts as a class. Students then spend time gathering their information. Encourage them to use different sources to collect their information from, e.g. books, magazines, newspapers, the Internet, etc. Students gather pictures of their favourite singer/band at this stage because they will need these in Exercise 1c.

(b) If you have access to a computer, students can type this up. Students can appoint a secretary who is responsible for writing down all the sentences. Alternatively, each student could write a sentence of their own. Students now write a short text based on the presentation text about their favourite singer/band. Encourage them to answer all the questions from Exercise 1a and to divide the text up as in the presentation text.

(c) Give each group a large piece of card or paper to make a poster. If students have not already collected their pictures then give them time to do this now. Each group then arranges their pictures and text and sticks them onto the poster.

(d) Students bring in a tape or CD with a song by their favourite singer/band.

2 Prepare the presentation

(a) Students discuss how they are going to present their poster, e.g. they can choose a spokesperson or they can each take a turn to read out a piece of information. Students practise their presentation in their group.

(b) Each group presents their poster to the class. If students want, they can finish their presentations by playing a song by their favourite singer/band.

> OPTIONAL ACTIVITY
> Students can vote for the best presentation. All the posters can be displayed on the classroom walls.

Project 2

Warm up

You may find it useful to bring in some examples of tourist leaflets for students' own town. Divide the class into groups of three or four.

1 Do your research

(a) **Stronger classes:** This part of the project can be set for homework. Each student can research the questions and then bring in the information they have collected to discuss in their group.

Weaker classes: Read through the prompt questions as a class and elicit suggestions and write them on the board. Students then research the questions further.

Encourage students to use different sources to collect their information from, e.g. books, magazines, newspapers, the Internet, etc. and to gather pictures at this stage because they will need these in Exercise 1b. Students then write notes for each question based on the information they have gathered.

(b) If students have not already collected their pictures then give them time to do this now.

2 Make the leaflet

(a) Give each group a large piece of paper. Show students some of the real tourist leaflets if you have brought them in. Ask students to fold their paper into half, and then in half again. They can then cut the two folds at the bottom to make four separate pages. Alternatively, for smaller leaflets students can simply fold their paper in half to make two pages, and draw the map on page 1 only.

(b) Students read through the instructions. In groups, each student takes a turn to write up some of the information they have gathered. Monitor and check students are taking turns to do this and that they are putting the right information on the right pages. Students can then read out or demonstrate how their leaflet works to the rest of the class.

> OPTIONAL ACTIVITY
> Students can vote for the most interesting leaflet. If there is space, the leaflets can be displayed around the class.

(c) If there is time, ask groups to think of a quiz about their own town/city. Encourage them to write questions and to think about the kind of quiz they are going to write, e.g. are they going to give choices for answers, etc. If there's space, groups can transfer their quizzes onto their leaflets.

Stronger classes: They can use the information in their leaflets but encourage them to write other questions which are not based on information in their leaflets.

Weaker classes: Students can write their questions based on the information in their leaflets only.

Students can prepare their quizzes and then ask their questions to other groups.

Project 3

Warm up

Ask students what they like to do in their free time and elicit some suggestions.

1 Prepare the survey

Divide the class into groups of three or four.

(a) Students read through the topics. Encourage groups to choose one topic they all agree on for their survey.

(b) Students read through the example survey. Draw their attention to the formation of the questions and the types of questions to ask. Encourage each student in the group to come up with a question for the topic they selected in Exercise 1a and to write it down.

(c) Students then exchange information with another group and ask other students their questions, noting down the answers.

2 Write the report

(a) Read through the example as a class, drawing students' attention to the questions in Exercise 1b which were answered. Students give the information they found out to the other members of their group and write it down.

(b) Students can appoint a secretary at this point to note down the information they have gathered. Go through the example report as a class, reminding them that a report should only give the main pieces of information about the number of people and the activities they researched. Give students time to write out their reports and then read them out to the rest of the class.

┌ OPTIONAL ACTIVITY ══════════
Find out if there is one free time activity which is more popular than others with the class.

Project 4

Divide the class into groups of three or four.

Warm up

Ask students how they think their own town/city has changed over the last 50 years.

1 Do your research

(a) Read through the prompts as a class. Encourage groups to choose one or two topics to focus on for their own town/city.

Weaker classes: It may be better for students to choose only one topic idea.

(b) Students read through the example questions.

Stronger classes: Give them time to prepare their questions on their chosen topic areas.

Weaker classes: Elicit information about the topic they chose in Exercise 1a and write it on the board to help them with their questions.

(c) This part of the project can be set for homework. Encourage students to interview different people in their family and to note down or record their answers.

(d) Students do further research using the different sources mentioned and collect photos of their town/city 50 years ago.

2 Do the presentation

(a) Students put together all the information they have collected and decide which pieces they will use and how they will organise it. Students then write up (or type) the information they have selected and add any pictures or photos they have collected.

(b) Students then choose a spokesperson or they can decide to take turns to present their project. Students introduce their project to the rest of the class and present the information.

┌ OPTIONAL ACTIVITY ══════════
Students can vote for the best project and the projects can then all be displayed in the class.

Workbook key

1 I know!

1 **a** 1 Lucy 2 Alex 3 Amy 4 Rob

  b 1 your 2 I'm 3 is 4 Hello 5 name's

2 **a** 🔊 TAPESCRIPT
  1 Taxi!
  2 Here's your hamburger. Thanks.
  3 This is a good video.
  4 They're in the museum.
  5 I love football.
  6 Oh, that's the phone.
  7 Here's the restaurant.
  8 I'd like a sandwich, please.
  9 This is our TV.
  10 This is a nice hotel.

  3 j 4 a 5 e 6 h 7 i 8 b 9 d 10 g

  b 🔊 See tapescript for Exercise 2a.

  a museum b sandwich d TV e football
  g hotel h phone i restaurant j video

  c 2 board 3 door 4 chair 5 desk 6 pencil
  7 pen 8 notebook

3 **a** 2 pages 3 notebooks 4 sandwiches 5 cities
  6 taxis 7 nationalities

  b 2 5 cassettes
  3 3 men
  4 2 women
  5 6 children
  6 4 people

  c 2 a 3 an 4 a 5 a 6 an 7 an 8 a

4 3 ✓ 4 a boring book 5 a good team
  6 ✓ 7 a new car 8 a bad hotel

5 🔊 TAPESCRIPT/ANSWERS

  cheap, board, new, phone; hotel, football, people, boring;
  hamburger, expensive, video, museum

6 **a** 🔊 TAPESCRIPT

  Lucy is fourteen.

  b 🔊 TAPESCRIPT/ANSWERS
  1
  My name's Kevin Thompson – Thompson, that's
    T-H-O-M-P-S-O-N.
  Er ... and I'm from Blackburn. That's B-L-A-C-K-
    B-U-R-N.
  2
  Man OK, now can I have your name please?
  Julie Yes, I'm Julie Claymore. Julie C-L-A-Y-
    M-O-R-E.
  Man Julie Claymore, right. And your city?

  Julie I'm from Newcastle.
  Man Sorry, what was that?
  Julie Newcastle. That's N-E-W-C-A-S-T-L-E.
  Man Fine. Thanks very much.

7 **a** 2 eleven 3 fourteen 4 nine 5 five 6 twenty
  7 seventeen 8 twelve

  b 1 ninety
  2 thirty-two, sixty-four
  3 seventy-four, eighty-five
  4 seventy-five, seventy-two
  5 forty-one, forty-four

  c 🔊 TAPESCRIPT/ANSWERS
  1 13 hotels
  2 15 cassettes
  3 70 pencils
  4 14 chairs
  5 60 women
  6 80 pages

8 1 Thanks
  2 don't understand
  3 I can help you
  4 the answer
  5 I don't know
  6 How do you say
  7 that's right

9 **a** 3 cinema 4 museum 5 hamburger 6 hotel
  7 excellent 8 cheap

  b 4 English 5 excellent 6 good 7 hamburger
  8 hotel 9 museum 10 phone 11 pizza
  12 restaurant 13 sandwich 14 taxi 15 teacher
  16 video

10 🔊 TAPESCRIPT
  1 Look at the picture on page 27.
  2 Read the sentences on page 56.
  3 Listen to the cassette.
  4 Write the answers.
  5 Work with a partner. Ask and answer the questions.
  6 Repeat the words.

  3 a 2 b 6 c 4 d 5 f

11 2 F 3 F 4 T 5 F 6 T

Unit check

1 1 your 2 I'm 3 What's 4 don't 5 phone 6 I
  7 help 8 Thanks 9 page

2 2 a 3 c 4 c 5 b 6 b 7 b 8 c 9 a

3 2 It's ~~a~~ _an_ expensive CD.
  3 The two ~~woman~~ _women_ are Sally and Caroline.
  4 Four + twelve = ~~sixty~~ _sixteen_
  5 What's ~~you~~ _your_ name?

6 It's a new ~~cinemas~~ *cinema*.
7 He's an interesting ~~people~~ *person*.
8 Forty-nine + seven = ~~fivety-six~~ *fifty-six*
9 The homework is ~~in~~ *on* page 35.

2 She isn't American

1
(a) a 4 b 8 c 5 d 1 e 2 f 7 g 9 h 6 i 3

(b) 2 I'm 3 She's 4 He's 5 You're 6 It's
7 Richard's 8 Australia's 9 I'm; What's

(c) 2 he's 3 it's 4 you're 5 It's

(d) 2 You are not / You're not
3 He is not / He's not
4 She is not / She's not
5 It is not / It's not

(e) 3 It's not Japanese.
4 She's not the winner.
5 It's boring.
6 You're not a film star.
7 It's expensive.
8 You're a bad dog.

(f) 2 Is she British?
3 Are you from Istanbul?
4 Am I right?
5 Is it a big city?
6 Is Brad Pitt a good actor?

(g) 🔊 TAPESCRIPT/ANSWERS
1 Is she American?
2 Are you from Japan?
3 Is he a good footballer?
4 Is it a cheap restaurant?
5 Am I the winner?
6 Is Broadway in New York?
7 Is the hotel expensive?
8 Is Maria from Spain?
9 Are you a singer?
10 Is the answer on page 5?

2
(a) 2 Portugal 3 Belgium 4 Poland 5 Italy
6 Turkey 7 Brazil

(b) Italian, Australian, Turkish, Polish, American, British, Belgian

(c) 2 She's from Russia. She's Russian.
3 He's from Spain. He's Spanish.
4 She's from America. She's American.
5 He's from Japan. He's Japanese.
6 She's from Turkey. She's Turkish.

3 🔊 TAPESCRIPT/ANSWERS
1 It's Polish.
2 It's Australian.
3 She's in Russia.
4 He's from Germany.

5 He's Turkish.
6 I'm not from Canada.

4
(a) 2 e 3 c 4 a 5 f 6 d

(b) 1 Who 2 What 3 Where 4 What 5 Where
6 Who 7 How 8 What

5 2 British (English) 3 She's 4 French 5 Italian 6 isn't

6
(a) Classroom things: pencil, chair, notebook, table;
Classroom verbs: write, look at, say, ask

(b) **Example answers**
Countries: Poland; Nationalities: Spanish, Chinese, Polish; Jobs: actor, teacher, footballer

7 2 T 3 F 4 T 5 T 6 F 7 T 8 F

8 are you
I'm; Wells
Is it
No; isn't
What's; address
best friend; he
he is
How; is
He's fifteen

Unit check

1 1 Belgium 2 is 3 from 4 isn't 5 Polish 6 Who's
7 Is 8 actor 9 teacher

2 2 b 3 c 4 c 5 a 6 c 7 b 8 c 9 a

3 2 Are you ~~Italyan~~ *Italian*?
3 ~~I not~~ *I'm not* a good singer.
4 ~~What~~ *What's* your address?
5 You ~~isn't~~ *aren't* an actor.
6 ~~Im~~ *I'm* from Poland.
7 Is he a ~~China~~ *Chinese* footballer?
8 ~~Maria is~~ *Is Maria* from Spain?
9 What ~~this is~~ *is this* in English?

3 We're a new band

1 2 Zoë f 3 Zoë e 4 Nick c 5 Zoë a 6 Nick b

2
(a) 2 You're 3 she's 4 It's 5 We're 6 You're
7 They're 8 He's

(b) 3 Tokyo isn't a city in China.
4 My favourite restaurant is/isn't expensive.
5 I'm not British. I'm …
6 Ferrari cars aren't cheap. They're expensive.
7 Ben Afleck isn't a sports star. He's a film star.
8 We're / We aren't in Rome.

(c) 2 e 3 b 4 g 5 f 6 h 7 c 8 a

(d) 2 Are Ken and Sandy American?
3 Am I a good singer?
4 Where are you from, Sarah?
5 Is the film interesting?
6 Are you and Robert football players?
7 Is Ricky Martin popular in Belgium?
8 Are Julia and I good actors?
9 Who are you?
10 What is your phone number?

(e) **Example answers**
2 Yes, I'm quite a good singer.
3 No, I'm not. I'm from Milano.
4 Yes, we are. We're in a really good band!
5 No, they aren't. They're cheap.
6 No, she isn't. She plays volleyball.
7 No, he isn't. He's American.
8 Yes, it's a very big school.

(f) 1 do 2 like 3 tennis 4 don't like 5 Do; like
6 No; don't

3 (a) 1 awful 2 fantastic 3 excellent 4 terrible

(b) **Example answers**
2 I really like mobile phones. I think they're fantastic.
3 I like tennis. I think it's excellent.
4 I really like hamburgers. I think they're great.
5 I like music. I think it's wonderful.
6 I don't like horses. I think they're awful.

4 1 her 2 him 3 them 4 you 5 it 6 me

5 (a) 🔊 TAPESCRIPT
think, singer, film, cinema, big, women;
see, please, read, museum, CD, people

(b) 🔊 TAPESCRIPT
1 Three big museums.
2 We think he's Swiss.
3 Fifteen CDs, please.
4 The Italian singer is the winner.

6 1 Guess what
2 really excited
3 want to go
4 Let's go together

7 (a) 1 'popular 2 A'merican 3 Japa'nese
4 'terrible 5 com'puter 6 'concert
7 seven'teen

(b) 'awful
'excellent
'boring
'interesting
ex'pensive

8 (a) 🔊 TAPESCRIPT
Hi! Welcome to my homepage. My <u>name</u> is Judy Dahrendorf. I live in Santa Cruz in California and I really like pop <u>music</u>. Can you guess who my <u>favourite</u> pop stars are? Yes, you're right: they're the Backstreet Boys. Here are four things I want to tell you about them:
• There are five people in the <u>band</u>: A.J. McLean, Howie Dorough, Nick Carter, Kevin Richardson and Brian Littrell.
• My favourite Backstreet Boy <u>is</u> A.J. McLean. I think he's <u>fantastic</u>! And he's a <u>wonderful</u> singer!
• My favourite BSB song is *I'll Never Break Your Heart*. All my friends say their favourite is *Quit Playing Games With My Heart*. (I think it's <u>really</u> good, but it isn't my favourite.)
• The Backstreet Boys are all <u>American</u>. Brian is from Kentucky, and the other four are <u>from</u> Florida.

Do you <u>like</u> my homepage? I hope so. And I hope you like the BSB too!

1 music 2 favourite 3 band 4 is 5 fantastic
6 wonderful 7 really 8 American 9 from
10 like

(b) 2 T 3 T 4 T 5 F 6 F

Unit check

1 1 from 2 she's 3 are 4 them 5 aren't
6 wonderful 7 film 8 together 9 we're

2 2 b 3 b 4 c 5 b 6 b 7 b 8 a 9 c

3 2 I think ~~he~~ *he's* an actor.
3 The pencils ~~isn't~~ *aren't* expensive.
4 *Are* John and Philip ~~are~~ from London?
5 No, they ~~not~~ *aren't* good friends.
6 This film is great. I like ~~him~~ *it* a lot.
7 ~~You like~~ *Do you like* this band?
8 Jim loves hamburgers, but I ~~don't like~~ *don't like* them.
9 ~~Are~~ *Is* rap music popular in your country?

(4) She likes Harry Potter

1 2 f 3 a 4 c 5 b 6 e .

2 (a) 1 speak 2 stop 3 understand 4 listen
5 learn 6 play 7 study 8 read 9 watch
10 live 11 write 12 work

(b) 2 watches 3 goes 4 speaks 5 listens
6 finishes 7 works 8 studies

(c) 2 writes 3 watch 4 play 5 speaks 6 live
7 understand

(d) 2 Sam doesn't like dogs but he likes cats.
3 Tony and Jill watch cartoons but they don't watch football.

4 We play tennis but we don't play computer games.

5 Julie doesn't listen to cassettes but she listens to CDs.

(e) 2 Does   3 Does   4 Do   5 Do   6 Do   7 Does

(f) 2 Do you always finish your homework? Yes, I do. / No, I don't.

3 Does your best friend like football? Yes, he/she does. / No, he/she doesn't.

4 Do you and your friends play volleyball? Yes, we do. / No, we don't.

5 Does your teacher speak English? Yes, he/she does. / No, he/she doesn't.

6 Do your friends understand Russian? Yes, they do. / No, they don't.

3 🔊 **TAPESCRIPT**

1 She likes it here.

2 Does Anna learn music?

3 Sam watches films.

4 She writes a lot of letters.

5 He lives in London.

6 The class finishes soon.

7 Paul speaks Italian.

2 /z/   3 /ɪz/   4 /s/   5 /z/   6 /ɪz/   7 /s/

4 **(a)** 2 cousin   3 brothers   4 grandmother   5 aunt   6 Barbara's   7 parents   8 Barbara's   9 David's

5 2 your   3 his   4 her   5 our   6 its   7 their

6 1 shop   2 house   3 hospital   4 car   5 washing machine   6 dishwasher

7 work: in a hospital; play: tennis, the piano; watch: television; write: an email, a letter; read: a book, a message; listen to: a band, your teacher

8 🔊 **TAPESCRIPT**

Uncle So tell me about your friend Rebecca. Her family lives in London, is that right?

Alice Yes, that's right. She lives in London with her mum and her two brothers. They're eight and ten. Her mother's a nurse – she works in a hospital.

Uncle And what are Rebecca's hobbies?

Alice Well, she reads a lot. She doesn't watch a lot of TV, but she really likes books.

Uncle And what do you do together, you and Rebecca? Do you go to concerts?

Alice No, we don't, but we go to the cinema, and we play music together a lot. Also, we go to the same school, so I often study with Rebecca at her house.

2 ✗   3 ✗   4 ✓   5 ✗   6 ✓   7 ✓

9 **Example answer**

Mateo's sister is Sonia and his brother is Marco. They're twelve and nine. His father works in a shop. Mateo's best friend is Franco. Mateo and Franco don't play tennis, but they play football together. Mateo speaks Italian and English.

Unit check

1 1 live   2 their   3 doesn't   4 Tara's   5 learn   6 speaks   7 volleyball   8 have   9 don't

2 2 b   3 b   4 a   5 a   6 b   7 c   8 c   9 c

3 2 Her father ~~speak's~~ *speaks* Japanese.

3 Sally and Frank ~~learns~~ *learn* French at school.

4 ~~Richards~~ *Richard's* sister plays tennis.

5 My cousin doesn't ~~works~~ *work* in a factory.

6 Do you like ~~me~~ *my* bicycle?

7 We ~~not~~ *don't* understand this question.

8 ~~Your father listens~~ *Does your father listen* to pop music?

9 Yes, he is my ~~friend~~ *friend's* uncle.

(5) # Where's the café?

1 1 museum   2 tube   3 boat   4 travel   5 river   6 eye   7 concert   8 market

2 **(a)** 🔊 **TAPESCRIPT/ANSWERS**

1 139   2 318   3 651   4 807   5 714   6 10,000   7 2,924

(b) 🔊 **TAPESCRIPT/ANSWERS**

1 Twelve and thirty = forty-two

2 Fifty and twenty-five = seventy-five

3 Eleven and eighty-nine = (one/a) hundred

4 A hundred and ten and a hundred and sixty = two hundred and seventy

5 Two hundred and sixty-six and seventeen = two hundred and eighty-three

6 Three hundred and nine and a hundred and ninety-eight = five hundred and seven

3 🔊 **TAPESCRIPT/ANSWERS**

1 I think he's thirty. /θ/

2 That's their father. /ð/

3 They buy clothes together. /ð/

4 Thanks for the birthday party. /θ/

4 **(a)** 1 's   2 are   3 are   4 's   5 's   6 are

(b) 1 there isn't   2 There are   3 there's   4 there aren't   5 There isn't   6 there's   7 There are   8 there's   9 There aren't   10 there isn't

5 **(a)** a 4   b 5   c 2   d 6   e 1   f 8   g 3   h 7

(b) **Example answers**

2 Is there a big post office in your town? Yes, there is.

3 Are there any bookshops near your school? No, there aren't.

4 Is there a good library in your school? Yes, there is.

5 Is there a railway station near your home? No, there isn't.

6 Are there any newsagents in your street? No, there aren't.

6 1 Listen to me. 2 Turn right. 3 Sit down. 4 Look!
5 Turn left. 6 Go home.

7 **a** 2 The park is behind the post office.
3 The supermarket is opposite the library.
The chemist is near / next to the supermarket.
4 The bank is on the corner. The restaurant is
between the bank and the newsagent.

b He wants to go to the chemist and the bookshop.

c 1 there is 2 down East Street 3 right
4 on the corner

8 1 Are you sure 2 You're welcome 3 Wait a minute
4 I have no idea

10 **a** 2 supermarket 3 Dixon's 4 Cycletech
5 bookshop

b 2 No, there aren't. 3 Yes, they do. 4 No, there
isn't. 5 No, they don't. 6 No, she isn't. 7 Yes,
there are. 8 Yes, there is.

Unit check

1 1 are 2 between 3 newsagent 4 underground
5 opposite 6 takes 7 aren't 8 there's 9 market

2 2 c 3 c 4 a 5 c 6 b 7 b 8 b 9 a

3 2 Excuse me, ~~there's~~ is there a library near here?
3 There aren't ~~a~~ any cheap CDs in this shop.
4 Is there a garden ~~on~~ in front of the house?
5 Go to the post office and ~~buys~~ buy a stamp.
6 ~~Is~~ Are there any good bookshops in this town?
7 Go straight on and turn ~~to left~~ left.
8 The café's ~~next~~ next to the post office.
9 There ~~isn't~~ aren't any factories near the river.

6 # They've got brown eyes

1 1 four 2 brown 3 She hasn't got 4 likes 5 forest
6 stupid

2 **a** 1 c 2 d 3 b 4 a

b 2 have got 3 's got 4 've got 5 've got
6 's got 7 's got 8 have got

c 2 Tom hasn't got a mobile phone.
3 Jessie and Tom haven't got a big family.
4 Tom's got a CD player.
5 Jessie's got brown hair.
6 Jessie and Tom have got brown eyes.
7 Tom hasn't got a computer.
8 Jessie's got a computer.

d 2 Has, got; Yes, he has
3 Have, got; No, I haven't
4 Has, got; No, she hasn't
5 Have, got; Yes, they have
6 Has, got; No, he hasn't

e **Example answers**
1 I've got long fingers.
2 My English teacher hasn't got fashionable clothes.
3 My best friend's got a nice smile.
4 My parents haven't got an old car.

3 **a** 2 red 3 black 4 blue 5 brown 6 white
7 yellow

b 1 ear 2 eye 3 face 4 hair 5 mouth 6 nose
7 arm 8 hand 9 finger 10 thumb 11 leg
12 foot

c 1 blond 2 eyes 3 nose 4 smile
5 good-looking 6 green 7 wavy

d 1 d 2 a 3 f 4 c 5 g 6 e 7 b

e 🔊 TAPESCRIPT
Now, I just need to get some details from you.
What's your first name?
Right, and your surname?
Ah ... how do you spell that, please?
Thanks. Now, how old are you?
And what's your address?
Sorry, can you repeat that, please?
OK, fine. And what's your phone number?
And your mobile number?
Right, that's it, then. We'll send you your membership
card in the next day or two ...

4 🔊 TAPESCRIPT
1 They've got wavy hair.
2 We've got twelve TVs.
3 Travel cards aren't very expensive.
4 He gives five interviews every day.
5 Vivien drives to the university.

5 1 hamster 3 snake 4 budgie 5 rabbit 6 spider
7 guinea pig 8 lizard 9 cat

6 Adjectives for hair: curly, straight, dark, fair; Other adjectives:
interesting, boring, cheap, expensive, intelligent, stupid

7 🔊 TAPESCRIPT
Sarah Who's this? In the photo?
Joe What photo? Oh – that's my sister's new boyfriend.
Sarah Oh yeah? What's his name?
Joe Gilles.
Sarah What was that?
Joe Gilles – G-I-double L-E-S. He's Swiss, but his family lives
over here now.
Sarah Swiss, right. So he speaks German.
Joe No, he doesn't – he speaks French. He comes from
Geneva. They speak French in that part of Switzerland.
Sarah How old is he?
Joe He's 21.
Sarah He's got nice eyes. Are they green? It's a small photo.
Joe No, they're blue. Look – you can see.
Sarah Oh yeah, they're blue. He's quite good-looking, isn't he?
Joe Oh, he's all right, I guess. Nothing special.
Sarah Yes, he is! He's got really nice fair hair.
Joe Yeah, well my sister thinks he's fantastic. She never stops
talking about ...

2 Swiss   4 French   5 21   6 blue   7 fair

8 (**a**) Picture 3

(**b**) 2 No, he hasn't. He's got short black hair.
3 No, they aren't. They're from Hong Kong.
4 Yes, she has. She works in a restaurant.
5 No, she doesn't. She works in a library.
6 No, he doesn't. He studies computer science.

Unit check

1 1 isn't   2 he's   3 wavy   4 clothes   5 good-looking
6 haven't   7 fair   8 eyes   9 wears

2 2 a   3 c   4 b   5 b   6 a   7 b   8 b   9 c

3 2 My friend ~~have~~ *has* got a guinea pig.
3 ~~Does she get~~ *Has she got* wavy hair?
4 ~~Where's~~ *What's* your address?
5 Tony and Joe ~~has~~ *have* got blue eyes.
6 Karen ~~haven't~~ *hasn't* got a computer.
7 ~~Why~~ *How* do you spell your surname, please?
8 ~~Are~~ *Have* you got a mobile phone?
9 No, I ~~don't~~ *haven't* got a little brother.

(7) This is delicious!

1 1e grasshopper   2c kangaroo   3d rattlesnake
4b alligator   5a snail

2 (**a**) 🔊 TAPESCRIPT/ANSWERS
1 lamb   2 tomatoes   3 eggs   4 chicken
5 onions   6 bananas   7 cheese   8 apples
9 grapes   10 potatoes   11 salt   12 strawberries
13 beef   14 carrots   15 sugar

a 6   b 5   c 13   d 15   e 8   f 12   g 14   h 4
i 11   j 2   k 1   l 10   m 3   n 9   o 7

(**b**) Fruit: apples, strawberries, grapes;
Vegetables: carrots, tomatoes, potatoes;
beef, chicken, lamb; salt, eggs, cheese

3 (**a**) Countable: onion, carrot, apple;
Uncountable: cheese, salt, sugar

(**b**) 2 C, U   3 U, C   4 U, C   5 C, U   6 C, U   7 U, C

(**c**) 2 some   3 an   4 a; some   5 some; some   6 a; a
7 some; an

(**d**) 2 some chips   3 an egg   4 some tomatoes
5 some honey   6 some bread   7 an ice cream
8 some water

(**e**) 1 that   2 these   3 This   4 Those   5 This
6 that

(**f**) 1 Can I help you?   2 I'd like   3 Would you like
4 I'd like   5 Would you like

(**g**) 1 Are you ready to order?
2 Yes, I'd like roast chicken please.
3 Would you like vegetables or salad?
4 I'd like vegetables please.
5 What would you like to drink?
6 Orange juice please.
7 Would you like anything else?
8 No thank you.

4 (**a**) 🔊 TAPESCRIPT
1 The Swiss waiter's got wavy hair.
2 We want some white wine.
3 William's got a wonderful dishwasher.
4 Would you like some water with your
sandwich?

(**b**) 🔊 TAPESCRIPT/ANSWERS
1 Which answer is correct?
2 What's wrong with you?
3 Who's the winner?
4 Where does Wendy write letters?

5 1 I'm really hungry   2 Do you think so   3 What's wrong

6 (**a**) a/an potato, lettuce, mushroom;
some water, meat, mayonnaise

7 (**a**) 🔊 TAPESCRIPT
Martin Mum. I'm hungry. Can I have a sandwich?
Mum OK. What do you want? Chicken? There's
some nice chicken here.
Martin No, not chicken. Are there any other things?
Mum Well, let's see …
Martin What about some roast beef?
Mum No, sorry. I used the beef for your father's
lunch.
Martin Oh, OK.
Mum We've got some cheese here. You can have a
cheese sandwich.
Martin Yeah, right. A cheese and salad sandwich –
that sounds good.
Mum Cheese and salad? No, sorry, that's a problem.
We haven't got a lettuce. How about … cheese
and tomato?
Martin Yeah, OK. And some mayonnaise?
Mum Yes, that's not a problem. So – a cheese and
tomato sandwich with mayonnaise, right?
Martin That's great. But don't worry, Mum – I can
make it myself.

2 ✗   3 ✓   4 ✗   5 ✓   6 ✓

(**b**) A cheese and tomato sandwich with mayonnaise.

Unit check

1 1 meal   2 meat   3 vegetables   4 fruit   5 dessert
6 have   7 sandwiches   8 an   9 some

2 2 a   3 b   4 b   5 c   6 a   7 a   8 b   9 c

3 2 ~~I like~~ *I'd like* a kilo of tomatoes, please.
3 They have some ~~waters~~ *water* with their meal.

4 I want to buy ~~a~~ *some* fruit at the market.
5 Mum wants some ~~egg~~ *eggs* from the shop.
6 Come and look at ~~this~~ *these* lovely strawberries!
7 I don't eat a lot of ~~sugars~~ *sugar*.
8 ~~You like~~ *Would you like* some cheese before the dessert?
9 I love ~~this~~ *that* car over there.

8 I sometimes watch soaps

1 2 black   3 shopping   4 doesn't drive   5 Australia
6 at home   7 watches   8 hardly ever

2 **(a)** Weekdays: Tuesday, Wednesday, Thursday, Friday;
Weekend: Saturday, Sunday

(b) 2 On Thursday.   3 On Monday.   4 On Sunday.
5 On Tuesday.   6 On Wednesday.   7 On Saturday.

(c) **Example answers**
1 I play tennis with my friend on Monday.
2 I have a guitar lesson on Wednesday.
3 I go shopping with my parents on Saturday.
4 I do my homework on Sunday.

3 **(a)** 1 always   2 often   3 usually   4 sometimes
5 hardly ever

(b) 2 Robert often plays football with his friends.
3 Tony and Philip are never on the school bus.
4 Beth hardly ever listens to classical music.
5 We always have pizzas on Friday.
6 The music is usually fantastic on this programme.
7 My parents sometimes help me with my
   homework.

(c) **Example answers**
1 I often go swimming on Sunday.
2 I sometimes have a burger at lunchtime.
3 I never go to bed before ten o'clock.
4 I usually listen to the radio in bed.
5 I hardly ever watch TV before school.

(d) 2 He plays football twice a week / at the weekend.
3 He writes letters once a week / on Sunday.
4 He walks to school five times a week.

(e) 2 Julie buys a newspaper seven times a week /
   every day.
3 Danny goes to the supermarket twice a week.
4 Denise goes to the cinema three times a month.
5 Greg goes to Paris / France once a year.

4 **(a)** soap opera; chat show; comedy; cartoon; game show;
documentary; sports programme

(b) 2 sports programme   3 news   4 cartoon
5 soap opera   6 comedy   7 game show
8 documentary

5 **(a)** 🔊 TAPESCRIPT/ANSWERS
1 'breakfast   2 'weekday   3 'lunchtime
4 'homework   5 'strawberry   6 'grasshopper
7 'rattlesnake   8 'girlfriend

6 **(a)** 2f It's six fifteen.   3e It's six fifty.   4c It's seven ten.
5d It's seven forty-five.   6a It's seven thirty-five.

(b) 🔊 TAPESCRIPT
1 What's the time? Er ... it's five to twelve.
2 Oh, look at the time! It's half past eight!
3 What time does the bus arrive? At ten past five.
4 School finishes at quarter to four.
5 Come on! The concert begins at nine o'clock.
6 When does the train leave? At twenty-five
   to eleven.

2 8.30   3 5.10   4 3.45   5 9.00   6 10.35

7 1 lives   2 north   3 hours   4 programmes   5 sometimes
6 doesn't   7 hardly ever

8 **(b)** Nouns: sandwiches, coffee, clothes; Verbs: buys, has,
makes; Adjectives: black, delicious, expensive; Adverbs:
never, sometimes, always

(c) **Example answers**
Sam sometimes buys expensive CDs.
Jill never watches boring programmes.
Jack usually enjoys expensive pizzas.
Rosa always drives new cars.

9 **(a)** 1 Television in a British family

(b) 2 No, he doesn't.
3 Jamie likes cartoons and comedies.
4 Yes, he does.
5 Kim's favourite programmes are soaps.
6 She watches films at the weekend.
7 They watch football matches together.

10 **(a)** 🔊 TAPESCRIPT

Boy Excuse me. Can I ask you some questions
about TV?
Woman Er ... oh yes, OK.
Boy How often do you watch TV?
Woman Not very often.
Boy For example – twice a week? Three times
a week?
Woman Erm ... I think four times a week, usually.
Yes. I hardly ever watch TV at the weekend.
Boy OK. Thanks. And, what do you watch – what
kinds of programmes?
Woman Well, I usually watch comedies. And
documentaries. I sometimes look at
documentaries about animals and science.
Boy Fine. OK. And what about soaps?
Woman No, never! They're terrible!
Boy Uh huh. And the news?
Woman No, I hardly ever watch the news. I read
a newspaper.
Boy OK – thank you very much.
Woman You're welcome.

She usually watches television four times a week.

(b) 🔊 documentaries: sometimes;   soaps: never;
the news: hardly ever

Unit check

1 1 at   2 usually   3 on   4 comes   5 soap   6 days
7 news   8 do   9 every

2 2 b   3 a   4 b   5 b   6 a   7 c   8 b   9 c

3 2 I have lunch at 1 o'clock every ~~days~~ *day*.
3 Students don't go to school ~~in~~ *at* the weekend.
4 We ~~watch always~~ *always watch* the news on TV.
5 They play tennis ~~two times~~ *twice* a month.
6 Does your mother ~~go sometimes~~ *sometimes go* to the market?
7 Patrick ~~doesn't never help~~ *never helps* his parents at home.
8 George and Sam ~~usually are~~ *are usually* in bed before 11 o'clock.
9 Carla has a music lesson ~~one~~ *once* a week.

(9) Don't close the door!

1 🔊 TAPESCRIPT

Anna All right, all right. Hang on a minute. I'm coming. Oh, it's you! What do you want?
Martin Don't close the door, Anna. I just want to talk to you.
Anna Oh Martin. Go away! Leave me alone!
Martin Anna, don't shout, please. Look – you're angry. I know that.
Anna Angry? Of course I'm angry! Go away. I don't want to talk to you!
Martin I know. But please, read this letter.
Anna All right. Give it to me. Now leave me alone.

1 want   2 door   3 talk   4 angry   5 away   6 read
7 Give   8 alone

2 (a) 1 cry   2 laugh   3 shout   4 be

(b) 1 Write   2 Don't eat   3 Don't sit   4 Go   5 Talk
6 Listen   7 Ask   8 Don't tell

(c) 2 Don't open the window.
3 Look at the kangaroos.
4 Don't switch on the TV.
5 Don't talk in the library.
6 Go to bed.

3 🔊 TAPESCRIPT/ANSWERS
1 I don't know why she isn't here.
2 <u>Don't</u> leave now.
3 Don't eat all the chocolate!
4 Please don't ask a lot of questions.
5 I don't understand why he's so angry.
6 Stop the music. I <u>don't</u> like it.
7 Don't open the box.
8 I <u>don't</u> think it's a good idea.

4 (a) 1 scared   2 happy   3 angry   4 excited   5 sad
6 confused   7 bored   8 worried

(b) 2 bored   3 happy   4 confused   5 excited
6 worried   7 unhappy   8 angry

(c) 🔊 TAPESCRIPT
1 Sunday! It's terrible. I've got nothing to do, and it's raining and I can't go out. I don't think there's anything on TV at the moment, is there? Let me have a look …
2 Oh, that's wonderful! Oh, I can't believe it – that's fantastic! A trip to New York! I'm going to New York! What a fantastic prize!
3 No, no, hang on a minute. That can't be right. Three hundred and sixty-two, multiplied by thirty-three, and then … No, that's not right. Um … three hundred, plus sixty-two, <u>divided</u> by thirty-three … Oh, this work is really hard! I'm going to stop and try again tomorrow.
4 John, it's half past eleven and Maria isn't home yet. It isn't like her. She's usually home by 10.30. And she hasn't got her mobile with her so I can't ring her …
5 Grrrr, this is awful! This stupid computer! What's wrong with it? It's so slow! Oh, come on, you stupid thing – this is driving me crazy!

2 Speaker 2 is excited because she's the winner of a trip to the USA.
3 Speaker 3 is confused because the homework is difficult.
4 Speaker 4 is worried because it's late and her daughter isn't home.
5 Speaker 5 is angry because there's a problem with the computer.

(d) 1 boring   2 worried   3 confusing   4 excited

5 1 she's fine   2 What's the matter   3 she misses

6 Example answers
I feel scared in the dark.
I feel worried about the test tomorrow.
I feel happy when I see you.

7 1 T   2 F   3 F   4 F   5 T   6 T   7 F

Unit check

1 1 happy   2 fine   3 matter   4 angry   5 boyfriend
6 listen   7 don't   8 help   9 worried

2 2 a   3 c   4 b   5 c   6 b   7 c   8 a   9 c

3 2 Come in and ~~you close~~ *close* the door.
3 ~~Not~~ *Don't* park in front of the post office, please.
4 I'm worried ~~for~~ *about* my test tomorrow.
5 ~~What~~ *What's* the matter?
6 Hang ~~up~~ *on* a minute! I'm coming.
7 How ~~you feeling~~ *are you feeling* today?
8 It's OK. ~~Be not~~ *Don't be* scared.
9 We're ~~boring~~ *bored* – there's nothing to do.

10 We can't lose

1 1 works 2 uses 3 take part 4 pushes 5 swim
6 pulls 7 ride 8 sits

2 **(a)** 2 He can't swim.
3 They can play tennis.
4 She can't dance.
5 She can read.
6 They can't ride a bike.

(b) 2 Can you swim? Yes, I can. / No, I can't.
3 Can you play tennis? Yes, I can. / No, I can't.
4 Can you dance? Yes, I can. / No, I can't.
5 Can you read? Yes, I can. / No, I can't.
6 Can you ride a bike? Yes, I can. / No, I can't.

(c) 2 can; can't walk 3 can 4 can't ride 5 Can; No;
can't 6 Can; can; can't

(d) **Example answers**
1 I can't juggle, but I can walk on my hands.
2 I can ride a bike, but I can't drive a car.
3 My parents can send an email, but they can't send
a text message.
4 My best friend can sing, but he/she can't dance.
5 A chimpanzee can't speak, but it can climb trees.
6 Young children can go to school, but they can't go
to work.

3 **(a)** 🔊 TAPESCRIPT/ANSWERS
1 Can you read? Yes, I can.
2 Can they <u>write</u>? Yes, they <u>can</u>.
3 Can she <u>play</u> the <u>guitar</u>? <u>Yes</u>, she <u>can</u>.

(b) 🔊 TAPESCRIPT/ANSWERS
1 I can <u>dance</u>, but I can't <u>sing</u>.
2 He can <u>read</u>, but he can't <u>write</u>.
3 Can she <u>play</u> the <u>piano</u>?
4 Can you <u>speak</u> <u>Spanish</u>?

4 **(a)** 2 snowboard 3 play tennis 4 ride; horse
5 rollerblades 6 swim 7 ski 8 play basketball

(b) go swimming, go snowboarding; play basketball, play
volleyball, play football; do gymnastics

5 **(a)** 2 Kevin likes playing tennis. He loves playing
volleyball, but he doesn't like horse-riding. He
hates doing gymnastics.
3 Brian and Louise like reading. They love playing
computer games, but they don't like playing the
guitar. They hate dancing.

(b) **Example answers**
1 I like cycling. I love going to the cinema, but I
don't like watching TV. I hate singing.
2 My best friend likes dancing. He/She loves
sending emails, but he/she doesn't like writing
letters. He/She hates doing homework.
3 My mother likes listening to music. She loves
playing tennis, but she doesn't like watching tennis
on TV. She hates walking the dog.

4 My brother likes playing the trumpet. He loves
going to concerts, but he doesn't like visiting his
grandparents. He hates getting up in the morning.

6 **(a)** a 5 b 4 c 2 d 1 e 6 f 3

(b) Miriam: netball, hockey, tennis, football; Jack: football,
rugby, cricket, tennis

7 **(a)** /æ/ camel, gymnastics, fantastic; /ɑː/ part, grass, laugh;
/eɪ/ rollerblade, strange, late

(b) **Example answers**
/ɪ/ miss, cricket, win, winter
/iː/ feel, leave, need, sleep
/ɒ/ hang on, holiday, hockey, oxygen
/əʊ/ go, rollerblading, snowboarding, boat

8 🔊 TAPESCRIPT
1 Tom never plays football – he doesn't like playing
team games. But he sometimes runs in the morning
and he likes doing gymnastics.
2 A: Can Cristina ride a bike?
B: Yes, she's really good at cycling. But she can't
ride a horse, and I don't think she can rollerblade.
3 A: What do you do in the winter, Matt?
B: Well, I don't like snowboarding, but I often go
skiing.
A: What about football?
B: No, I think football's boring.
4 A: Pete, can you sing?
B: Me? Oh, I'm a terrible singer! I love music,
though. I can play the guitar and I'd like to learn
the violin.

2 A 3 B 4 B

9 **(a)** 🔊 TAPESCRIPT
Interviewer Today in the studio we're talking to Mark
Cavalcanti. Mark is only 17 but he's already a star in
British tennis. Mark, good morning.
Mark Good morning.
Interviewer Now Mark, your family name's interesting
– Cavalcanti.
Mark That's right. My grandfather's Italian.
Interviewer So can you speak Italian?
Mark I can understand some things but no, I can't
speak it really. My parents grew up here in Britain so
I'm British and we only talk in English at home.
Interviewer And is tennis the only sport in your life?
Mark No, not at all. I love swimming, and it's great
exercise.
Interviewer Are you a good swimmer?
Mark Well, I'm OK. I like basketball too. I sometimes
play in a local team. But my first love is tennis.
Interviewer Are there any other tennis players in your
family?
Mark No, not really. My mother Helen loves watching
sport, but she doesn't do any sport herself. And then

there's Anna, my sister – she's 13 and she's really good at running. She wins all her races at school.

Interviewer Great! But now let's talk about your tennis. There's a big match coming up in Australia ...

1 17 2 English 3 British 4 tennis 5 swimming
6 basketball 7 sister 8 watching sport 9 running

Unit check

1 1 hockey 2 team 3 swim 4 races 5 free 6 can
7 loves 8 guitar 9 doesn't

2 2 a 3 b 4 c 5 c 6 a 7 a 8 a 9 b

3 2 ~~Maria can she~~ *Can Maria* use a computer?
3 We love ~~watch~~ *watching* sports programmes on TV.
4 Sorry, I ~~can~~ *can't* come to your party on Saturday.
5 My brother likes basketball and ~~snowboard~~ *snowboarding*.
6 Can your friends ~~swimming~~ *swim*?
7 Nick ~~not likes~~ *doesn't like* running, so he never plays tennis.
8 ~~Do you can~~ *Can you* play the violin?
9 I hate ~~play~~ *playing* hockey in the rain.

11 Reading on the roof!

1 1 T 2 F 3 F 4 T 5 F 6 F

2 **a** playing, doing, eating; writing, using, having; swimming, shopping, running

b 2 She's shopping 3 They're watching
4 I'm writing 5 They're sitting 6 We're doing
7 She's having

c 2 Alice isn't eating fish. She's eating chicken.
3 Dorothy isn't talking to George. She's sleeping.
4 Maria and Bill aren't listening to music. They're watching TV.
5 Pat isn't dancing. She's playing cards with Anne.
6 Wendy and Lisa aren't playing the guitar. They're singing.

d 2 Are you watching the news? No, I'm not.
3 Is Helen doing her homework? Yes, she is.
4 Are Ken and Neill playing tennis? No, they aren't.
5 Is Joe using the computer? No, he isn't.

e **Example answers**
1 I'm sitting in the classroom.
2 I'm studying English.
3 I'm using this book.
4 No, I'm sitting with my friend.
5 Yes, I'm wearing glasses.
6 My friends are listening to the teacher. Our teacher is talking to us.

f 2 I read; I'm reading
3 they're playing; They play
4 She's visiting; She often stays
5 He catches; isn't working

3 🔊 TAPESCRIPT
1 Harry's hobby is horse-riding.
2 I'm hardly ever hungry at home.
3 He's unhappy about his hair.
4 How often does Helen help you?
5 Hanna's having a hamburger at the Hilton Hotel.

4 **a** **Across:** 1 shower 3 armchair 6 window 7 bed
8 door 9 table
Down: 1 sofa 2 fridge 4 cooker 5 toilet
7 bath

b 1 living room 2 bathroom 3 bedroom
4 kitchen 5 hall

c 🔊 TAPESCRIPT
I've got a bed and a desk in my room. There's a small table next to the bed. The desk is under the window and I've got my computer on the desk. There's a small armchair in the corner of the room. On the wall between the desk and the armchair I've got three pictures of my favourite pop stars. The door is near the armchair.

1 next to 2 under 3 on 4 between 5 near

5 1 What are you up to
2 Come round to my place
3 I'm on my way
4 See you

7 **a** Sue: 1 ✗ 2 ✗ 3 ✓ 4 ✗ 5 ✓
Emma: 1 ✓ 2 ✓ 3 ✓ 4 ✗ 5 ✓

b 🔊 TAPESCRIPT
Dad Hello.
Emma Hi Dad. It's Emma.
Dad Emma! Hello, love. Where are you?
Emma We're in Empoli right now. We're staying in a beautiful hotel here – it's a really nice place.
Dad So you're having a good time?
Emma Oh yeah. And I'm speaking a lot of Italian now. It's great when people understand me – I'm feeling good about saying things in Italian now.
Dad That's excellent. And is the food nice?
Emma Fantastic! We all love the food here, and it's not only pizza. We're having great meals.
Dad And what about the weather? Is it still raining? It's sunny here in England.
Emma Oh, well it's still raining here and it's cold. But that's OK. We're still having a good time. Listen, Dad, I must go now. Some other people want to use the phone.
Dad OK, love. But ring again on Friday, all right?
Emma Yes, I will. Is everyone OK at home?
Dad Yes, we're fine.
Emma Well, give them my love. Bye, Dad.
Dad Bye.

Unit check

1 1 bedroom 2 finishing 3 is 4 are 5 living
6 reading 7 in 8 aren't 9 they're

2 2 c 3 a 4 b 5 c 6 c 7 c 8 a 9 b

3 2 The weather is good and we ~~stay~~ *'re staying* in a nice hotel.
3 What's happening? Is our team ~~wining~~ *winning*?
4 No, they ~~not~~ *aren't* playing well today.
5 ~~I not wear~~ *I'm not wearing* my glasses at the moment.
6 What ~~Kate is~~ *'s Kate* doing?
7 She's ~~rideing~~ *riding* her new bike.
8 Don't make a noise – your grandfather ~~sleeps~~ *is sleeping*.
9 This shop ~~is always selling~~ *always sells* delicious ice cream.

12 Can I try them on?

1 1 festivals 2 national holiday; clothes 3 parade; balloons
4 carnival; dance; colourful

2 **(a)** 1 August 2 December 3 April 4 October
5 June 6 May 7 February 8 November
9 March 10 September

(b) January; July

(c) [personal answers]

(d) [in the northern hemisphere] 1 winter 2 spring
3 summer 4 autumn

(e) Example answers
In winter I like going to the mountains.
In spring I clean my bedroom and I sometimes paint it.
In summer I love swimming in the sea.
In autumn I have new teachers at school.

3 1 in 2 at 3 at 4 in 5 on 6 on 7 in 8 in 9 in

4 **(a)** 2 jeans 3 scarf 4 trousers 5 shirt 6 jumper
7 T-shirt 8 socks 9 trainers 10 dress 11 jacket
12 shoes

(b) Example answers
1 I usually wear trousers and a jumper to school.
2 My favourite clothes are jeans and T-shirts.
3 I hate wearing a winter coat.
4 My best friend usually wears shorts in summer.
5 I buy my clothes in a shop in town.

5 **(a)** 🔊 TAPESCRIPT
1 sad   said
2 bad   bed
3 man   men
4 dad   dead
5 sat   set

(b) 🔊 TAPESCRIPT/ANSWERS
1 I'm sad.
2 You aren't in bed!
3 Look at the man.
4 Is it dead?
5 They sat together.

(c) 🔊 TAPESCRIPT
1 Annie is Alan's best friend.
2 I'm helping Joanna in December and January.
3 Emma's jacket is black and yellow.
4 How many magazines is Danny sending?

6 **(a)** 2 Can I have a banana?
3 Can I use your computer?
4 Can I play football with you?
5 Can I switch the television on / switch on the television?
6 Can I go to the toilet please?

(b) 2 Can I borrow your dictionary?; I'm using it.
3 Can I come round to your place?; We've got visitors.
4 Can I see your homework?; Here you are.
5 Can I wear your sunglasses?; They're really expensive.
6 Can I talk to you?; What's the problem?

(c) 1 ones 2 one 3 one 4 one 5 ones; ones
6 ones; ones

7 1 f 2 e 3 g 4 c 5 a 6 b 7 h 8 d

8 **(a)** Ticks for 1; 2; 3; 4; 7

(b) Friday; Dave; Japanese; August; Tuesday; April

9 🔊 TAPESCRIPT
Assistant Can I help you?
Nadia Yes, I'm interested in a dress in the window.
Assistant Yes – which one are you looking at?
Nadia It's over there behind the shirts – next to that black jumper.
Assistant Oh, yes, the green one. That's a lovely dress.
Nadia How much is it?
Assistant It's ... £49.
Nadia Oh, OK. Can I try it on, please?
Assistant I'm afraid we haven't got many sizes in that dress. Only ten or sixteen. What size are you?
Nadia Twelve.
Assistant No, sorry, we haven't got a twelve. Is there anything else I can show you?
Nadia Well actually, those tops are nice. The pink one would look nice with my new trousers.
Assistant Yes, or you can wear it with jeans or a skirt.
Nadia OK, can I try it on, please?
Assistant Yes, of course. The changing room's over there ...

1 a 2 c 3 c 4 b 5 a

10 2 black 3 white 4 red 5 black 6 black
7 grey / dark blue

Unit check

1   1 clothes   2 costume   3 trousers   4 huge   5 in
     6 festival   7 parade   8 at   9 enjoy

2   2 c   3 a   4 b   5 b   6 c   7 a   8 b   9 c

3   2 Dan's birthday is ~~on~~ *in* February.
     3 ~~I can~~ *Can I* use your phone?
     4 Of ~~corse~~ *course* you can.
     5 Our garden is beautiful ~~at~~ *in* spring.
     6 Can I ~~borow~~ *borrow* your jacket?
     7 Sorry, you ~~can~~ *can't*. I want to wear it today.
     8 Can I try ~~up~~ *on* this dress, please?
     9 We always go shopping ~~the~~ *on* Saturday.

(13) He was only 40

1   1 e   2 f   3 a   4 b   5 d   6 c

2   **(a)**   1 was   2 was   3 was   4 were   5 were
           6 were   7 was   8 was   9 were   10 was
           11 were   12 were

     (b)   2 No, she wasn't. She was a film star.
           3 No, they weren't. They were very sad when she
             died.
           4 No, they weren't. They were comedies.
           5 No, it wasn't. It was Stan.
           6 No, they weren't. They were in black and white.

     (c)   2 Were Jane and Diana in the park at 2.30? Yes, they
             were.
           3 Was Julia in her bedroom at 9 o'clock? Yes, she was.
           4 Were Paul and Carol in the supermarket at 10.15?
             No, they weren't.
           5 Was Anna in the bookshop at 5.30? No, she wasn't.
           6 Was Matt in the kitchen at 1 o'clock? Yes, he was.

3   **(a)**   1 yesterday   2 last   3 last   4 yesterday   5 last

     (b)   **Example answers**
           1 I was in the bathroom at 8.15 yesterday morning.
           2 I was at my friend's house at 5 pm last Friday.
           3 Yes, I was.
           4 No, we weren't at school because yesterday was
             Sunday.
           5 No, I was at my friend's place last weekend.
           6 My birthday was on (Monday) last year.

4   🔊   TAPESCRIPT

Woman   Oh, I love that song.

Boy   I think I know it. Is it John Lennon?

Woman   That's right. He was my favourite. I remember
   the day he was shot. I was really sad.

Boy   When was that, Mum?

Woman   1980. December 1980. He wasn't very old – he was
   only 40.

Boy   What was the name of that band he was in? Before he
   was shot?

Woman   Oh, Tom – the Beatles!

Boy   Oh yes, right. Of course. Were they from London?
Woman   No they weren't! They were from Liverpool.

1 was   2 was   3 was   4 wasn't   5 was   6 was
7 Were   8 weren't   9 were

5   **(a)**   🔊   TAPESCRIPT/ANSWERS
           1 Were they in London? Yes, they were.
           2 Were they <u>happy</u>? <u>No</u>, they <u>weren't</u>.
           3 Were the <u>girls</u> at <u>home</u>? <u>Yes</u>, they <u>were</u>.
           4 Was he an <u>actor</u>? <u>Yes</u>, he <u>was</u>.
           5 Was she <u>worried</u>? <u>No</u>, she <u>wasn't</u>.
           6 Was <u>Dave</u> at <u>school</u>? <u>No</u>, he <u>wasn't</u>.

     (b)   🔊   TAPESCRIPT/ANSWERS
           1 <u>Helen</u> was in <u>hospital</u> on <u>Wednesday</u>.
           2 Our <u>parents</u> were at the <u>library</u> <u>yesterday</u>.
           3 <u>When</u> were you in <u>Paris</u>?
           4 <u>What</u> was your <u>address</u>?

6   **(a)**   12th, twelfth
           2, two, 2nd
           15, fifteen, 15th
           three, 3rd, third
           one, 1st, first
           fifty, fiftieth
           22nd, twenty-second
           thirty-one, 31st, thirty-first

     (b)   1 June   2 September   3 Friday   4 Sunday

     (c)   2 Our national holiday is on the third of July.
           3 Christmas Day is on the twenty-fifth of December.
           4 New Year's Day is on the first of January.
           5 The festival is on the ninth of October.
           6 My party was on the thirtieth of August last year.

7   1 Can I have a look   2 Oh brilliant   3 You must be joking
     4 Calm down

9   🔊   TAPESCRIPT
     1 the eleventh of December, two thousand and four
     2 the twenty-fifth of November, nineteen eighty
     3 the thirtieth of July, nineteen ninety-five
     4 the thirteenth of September, nineteen fifty-nine
     5 the thirty-first of August, nineteen ninety-nine
     6 the third of March, two thousand and one

     2 b   3 d   4 f   5 c   6 a

10   a 6   b 2   c 5   d 3   e 1   f 4

     2 London   3 In 1910.   4 In Hollywood.   5 Because there
     were no words or music.   6 In 1920.   7 *Modern Times*.
     8 In Switzerland.

Unit check

1   1 first   2 were   3 was   4 wasn't   5 way   6 afternoon
     7 recording   8 weren't   9 fifth

2   2 b   3 a   4 c   5 b   6 a   7 b   8 c   9 b

3 2 Anne's brothers ~~was~~ *were* in Paris last weekend.

3 Tom and I ~~wasn't~~ *weren't* here yesterday morning.

4 Where ~~you were~~ *were you* last Saturday?

5 There ~~was~~ *were* about 50 people at the party.

6 When ~~were~~ *was* Sara in Canada?

7 I was in bed at 10.30 ~~yesterday in the~~ *last* night.

8 ~~They were~~ *Were they* at school on Friday?

9 Was James in the bookshop ~~last~~ *yesterday* afternoon?

(14) She didn't listen

1 1 angry 2 terrible 3 dirty 4 hungry 5 different
6 clean 7 famous

2 (a) 2 visited 3 hated 4 studied 5 died 6 tried
7 travelled 8 arrived

(b) 2 arrived 3 visited 4 studied 5 travelled
6 died

(c) 2 Last night, Ben and Adam played cards. They didn't play tennis.

3 In 2002, Alan worked in a hospital. He didn't work in a restaurant.

4 Yesterday, I phoned my boyfriend. I didn't phone my mother.

5 On Friday, we didn't dance. We watched TV.

6 On Saturday, Mum parked in front of the library. She didn't park near the cinema.

(d) 2 didn't have 3 didn't phone 4 didn't switch on
5 didn't play 6 didn't close

3 (a) 🔊 TAPESCRIPT

liked, travelled, called, watched
hated, started, landed, wanted

/t/ or /d/: travelled, called, watched;
/ɪd/: started, landed, wanted

(b) 🔊 TAPESCRIPT

1 They visited a museum.

2 They landed on the moon.

3 The concert ended at 11 o'clock.

4 We waited at the station.

(c) 🔊 TAPESCRIPT/ANSWERS

1 We watched a film.

2 He lived in Barcelona. /d/

3 We helped Annie with her homework. /t/

4 They laughed at me. /t/

5 Sally stayed in a hotel. /d/

6 We opened our books. /d/

4 (a) **Example answers**

1 Yes, I enjoyed my breakfast.

2 No, I didn't cycle, I walked.

3 I arrived at 8.45.

4 It started at 9 o'clock.

5 I had (six) lessons.

6 Yes, I did.

7 We watched a football match on TV last night.

(b) 1 did you have; Did you like

2 did he die

3 did you do

4 Did they live

(c) 1 Yes, I had a great time.

2 Where did you go?

3 I travelled to Barcelona.

4 When did you get there?

5 I arrived on the 28th of July.

6 Did you stay with friends?

7 No, I stayed at the Hotel Metropol.

5 (a) 2 go 3 plays 4 have 5 having

(b) have: a good time, a meal, a fight, a wash, a swim;
play: the guitar, tennis, hockey, basketball, the violin;
go to: the bank, the shops, university, town, the toilet

6 1 d 2 c 3 f 4 a 5 b 6 e

7 (a) + ed: answered, played; + d: danced, practised;
+ ied: married, cried; double letter: stopped, travelled

(b) /t/: asked, watched, looked; /d/: travelled, enjoyed, died; /ɪd/: hated, wanted, ended

8 🔊 TAPESCRIPT

Sandro Hello

Tony Sandro, hi. It's Tony. I'm ringing from Cambridge.

Sandro Tony, hi! How are you?

Tony Fine! We arrived in London on Monday. The plane landed at 5.15 in the morning.

Sandro Oh dear!

Tony Yeah, really early. So we were in the city by 7.30. And we stayed in London for two nights.

Sandro Where? In a hotel?

Tony Yes, we were in a hotel for the first night. And then on Tuesday we stayed at my uncle's place.

Sandro So what was London like? What did you do?

Tony Well, we spent a lot of time at my uncle's house – talking, you know. But we went all round the city in a tourist bus – that was really good. And we went for a boat trip on the river. Dad wanted to visit the British Museum too, but we didn't have time for that.

Sandro So when did you leave for Cambridge?

Tony On Wednesday. We got the early evening train and now we're staying with my cousins. They've got a great house here. Anyway, Sandro – how are things? How's Carla? I tried to ring her yesterday but …

2 B 3 C 4 C 5 B

Unit check

1 1 on 2 in 3 studied 4 nurse 5 hospital
6 stopped 7 didn't 8 were 9 died

2 2 a 3 c 4 a 5 c 6 b 7 c 8 a 9 b

3 2 They ~~traveled~~ *travelled* to the USA in 2002.

3 Why ~~you did~~ *did you* open the window?

4 I ~~not wanted~~ *didn't want* to go swimming yesterday.

5 Where ~~she parked~~ *did she park* the car?

6 ~~John and Melanie enjoyed~~ *Did John and Melanie enjoy* the film last night?

7 No, they didn't ~~liking~~ *like* it at all.

8 I ~~tryed~~ *tried* to phone you, but you weren't at home.

9 Lisa and her family ~~was~~ *were* born in Spain.

15 Where did they go?

1 🔊 TAPESCRIPT

Interviewer Sandra Rivett? Who was she?

Professor She was the young woman who looked after Lord Lucan's children. And on November 7 1974, somebody killed her in a room in Lord Lucan's house.

Interviewer Lord Lucan? Did he kill her?

Professor Well, we don't know for sure, but many people think he did it. But we do know that Lord Lucan's wife, Lady Lucan, was in the house that day. She heard a noise and went downstairs. She opened the door, and saw Sandra dead. Then somebody tried to kill her too, and ran away. But Lady Lucan wasn't dead. The police think that Lord Lucan wanted to kill his wife, and killed Sandra Rivett by mistake.

1 woman 2 children 3 house 4 kill 5 know
6 wife 7 opened 8 tried 9 dead 10 killed

2
(a) **Across:** 1 left 3 became 4 ate 5 knew
7 saw 9 ran 11 thought 13 gave 14 took
Down: 2 found 3 began 6 wrote 8 went
10 had 12 got

(b) 1 saw 2 went; left 3 gave; thought 4 wrote; got 5 found; took

(c) 1 got up 2 took the dog / went
3 went shopping 4 got home
5 wrote a letter 6 had lunch

(d) 2 didn't give 3 didn't come 4 didn't become
5 didn't leave 6 didn't hear 7 didn't run
8 didn't go

(e) 1 When did it begin
2 Where did you go
3 Did George have
4 Did you sit
5 What did you have
6 Was it
7 When did you get

3 🔊 TAPESCRIPT/ANSWERS

1 Did she know the answer?
2 Did they <u>give</u> you a <u>present</u>?
3 <u>When</u> did he <u>write</u> to you?
4 <u>What</u> did she <u>think</u> of the <u>book</u>?
5 <u>Where</u> did you <u>get</u> your <u>jacket</u>?
6 <u>Why</u> did they <u>leave</u> on <u>Sunday</u>?

4
(a) 2 brilliantly 3 easily 4 nicely 5 unhappily
6 really 7 mysteriously 8 noisily

(b) 2 She wrote carefully.
3 He ran slowly.
4 She shouted angrily.
5 They walked quickly.
6 A ghost suddenly appeared .

(c) 2 quietly 3 brilliant 4 careful 5 easily
6 mysterious 7 unhappy 8 suddenly

(d) **Example answers**
Mr Brown probably had a surprise visitor.
Perhaps he had a phone call.
Maybe he was late for work.

5
2 Have you got your passport?
3 Are you tired?
4 Do you want me to have a look at it?
5 Are you feeling good?

7
1 F 2 F 3 T 4 T 5 T 6 F

Unit check

1
1 got 2 went 3 could 4 thought 5 had 6 know
7 looked 8 didn't 9 slowly

2
2 b 3 a 4 c 5 a 6 b 7 c 8 a 9 c

3
2 Sara ~~goes~~ *went* swimming yesterday afternoon.
3 He looked at her ~~angryly~~ *angrily* and left the room.
4 My grandfather ~~can~~ *could* juggle when he was young.
5 I ran ~~quick~~ *quickly* to the phone and called the police.
6 ~~You ate~~ *Did you eat* all the chocolate?
7 Ben ~~not said~~ *didn't say* goodbye to me.
8 ~~He didn't maybe~~ *Maybe he didn't* have time.
9 When ~~your parents got~~ *did your parents get* home last night?

16 Now and then

1
(a) 🔊 TAPESCRIPT

Grandfather When I was young, of course, we didn't even have television!

Grandfather I think school life is more difficult now, certainly.

Grandfather I think perhaps she's happier than I was!

Lucy Some things now are difficult for my granddad.

Lucy I'm sure that now life is faster than in the 1950s.

Lucy There are a lot more cars these days.

1 e 2 c 3 f 4 a 5 d 6 b

(b) young, old; crowded, empty; different, the same; fast, slow; difficult, easy; happy, sad

2
(a) 2 hotter 3 happier 4 more difficult 5 unhappier
6 more expensive 7 better 8 hungrier 9 more mysterious 10 worse

(b) 1 B 2 A 3 A 4 B 5 B

(c) 1 younger 2 taller 3 bigger 4 better
     5 worse 6 more interesting

(d) 2 The dress is more expensive than the shirt.
     3 The book is more interesting than the magazine.
     4 West Street is busier than Green Street.
     5 Marian's car is faster than Jack's.
     6 The CD is better than the cassette.

(e) **Example answers**
     1 My best friend is taller than me.
     2 My street is quieter than my friend's street.
     3 My town is better than my grandmother's town.
     4 School days are more boring than weekends.
     5 Comedy programmes are funnier than news
       programmes.
     6 History is more interesting than English.

3 🔊 TAPESCRIPT/ANSWERS
     1 She's <u>younger</u> than him.
     2 You're <u>happier</u> than me.
     3 The <u>bank</u> is <u>older</u> than the <u>bookshop</u>.
     4 <u>Maths</u> is more <u>difficult</u> than <u>Science</u>.
     5 The <u>book</u> was more <u>interesting</u> than the <u>film.</u>
     6 . The <u>shoes</u> were more <u>expensive</u> than the <u>trainers</u>.

4 (a) 1 f 2 g 3 d 4 h 5 e 6 c 7 a 8 b

   (b) 1 exciting 2 safe 3 old-fashioned 4 modern
        5 dangerous 6 noisy

5 (a) 2 The camps were at the seaside or in the
          countryside.
        3 They were noisier and less comfortable than
          Center Parcs.
        4 Center Parcs are bigger than Butlin's camps, but
          they're more expensive.
        5 People were freer to choose what they wanted
          to do at Center Parcs.
        6 At Center Parcs it's always warm at night.

7 🔊 TAPESCRIPT

I took this photo of my family last summer. My two
brothers are on the left – Frank and Tim. Frank's the one
with the curlier hair and he's a bit shorter than Tim.

That's my sister Anne on the other side – she's standing
next to her friend Lisa. You can see they're both tall and
they've got the same hair style. Lisa always wears more
expensive clothes than Anne, but I think Anne always
looks happier.

Then there's Dad here – he's playing cards with Uncle Bill.
Dad's younger than Uncle Bill but he looks older and he's a
bit fatter. And you can see he's winning the game because
he's a better card player.

So that's everyone. Oh, there are the cats too. The big one's
called Sandy. She's a bit boring – she just sleeps most of
the time. The little one with Uncle Bill is friendlier and
more interesting – he's called Pablo.

1 Frank 2 Tim 3 Lisa 4 Anne 5 Sandy
6 Uncle Bill 7 Dad 8 Pablo

8 **Example answer**
Alan's TV is more modern than Peggy's. His window is
smaller and the street outside his room is busier and noisier.
Peggy's chairs are older but more comfortable than Alan's.
Outside her room, she's got a lovely garden and it is quieter.
Her window is bigger.

Unit check

1 1 town 2 was 3 busier 4 more 5 crowded
     6 old-fashioned 7 difficult 8 modern 9 easier

2 2 c 3 b 4 a 5 a 6 c 7 b 8 b 9 c

3 2 I think English is ~~easyer~~ *easier* than German.
     3 Buses are ~~more cheaper~~ *cheaper* than trains.
     4 My mother is ~~more old~~ *older* than my aunt.
     5 It's hot today, but it was ~~hoter~~ *hotter* last week.
     6 My bike is good, but Sam's bike is ~~gooder~~ *better*.
     7 The jeans are ~~expensive than~~ *more expensive* than
       the trousers.
     8 Exercise 1 was OK, but Exercise 2 was ~~difficulter~~ *more
       difficult*.
     9 Oh no! This hotel's ~~more bad~~ *worse* than the last one!

Acknowledgements

The publishers are grateful to the following
contributors:

Annie Cornford: editorial work
Cheryl Pelteret: initial script writing

Pentacor Book Design: text design and layouts

Claire Thacker: final script writing